For you, the reader,
we hope you will be inspired in your own journey to life.

May this story carry you further towards love,
joy and peace, and reveal the truth of living,
which can sometimes be difficult to find.

ISBN: 978-1-0685587-6-4

Journey to Life

www.journeytolife.co.uk

journeytolife1@outlook.com

First published 2026 by Boz Publications Ltd

A CIP catalogue record for this book is available from the British Library.

BOZ PUBLICATIONS

Boz Publications Ltd.

71-75 Shelton Street, Covent Garden, London, WC2H 9JQ, United Kingdom.

www.bozpublications.com - office@bozpublications.com

JOURNEY TO LIFE

Rob and Jane - broken lives
shining a light of hope and healing

Beckie Welch

ACKNOWLEDGEMENTS

Having been given the opportunity to write this book, I have been astonished at the support that I have received. I would firstly like to thank Tim Murray, who suggested this venture to me alongside the encouragement that it was something I had the ability to achieve. I am grateful for the support and advice he has offered me throughout the project.

I would like to thank those who willingly gave their time to share their own personal experiences and stories of their time at Living Springs. You inspired me not only in my writing, but in my personal life, having witnessed the love and care you so obviously feel for others.

I would like to personally thank my loving husband, Matthew Welch, and our wonderful children, Zachary, Sophia, and Talia, who have generously given me the time to work on this project and have loved and supported me in this endeavour. I have been regularly encouraged by so many of my friends and family- too many to name, but all equally valued. You have all inspired me to believe in myself and to broaden my own horizons.

I am grateful to David Faulker and Adrian Lowe, who have supported me with the editing process; their feedback was invaluable to me. I also extend my thanks to Caroline Taylor and Jeremy Watson for the time they gave to proofreading.

Above all, I extend my absolute appreciation to Rob Chapman. I am privileged to have been trusted to portray Rob's personal journey, alongside the history of Living Springs. I must acknowledge that this book became more than a literary pursuit, forcing me to reflect on my own personal beliefs and experiences. There were so many times through writing this book that I felt in awe of the miracles that God had completed. And remarkable though they are in this story, that is not what drew me in.

Instead, I was drawn to the heart of a man who embodied so many of my own feelings that I couldn't help but be inspired. I have read many Christian books that have inspired and drawn me in with their miraculous stories, but in a way that felt unattainable. I was not one of those people destined for great things, walking in step with God and experiencing daily spiritual encounters; I grew to accept that it was a life which was reserved for others.

Yet, here sat a man in front of me who described the very nature of my own heart. The same longing to know God, but more importantly, the same lack of emotional connection and felt love of God that I so desired. It may seem odd that this should be what inspired me, but for me, it embodied a paradox that I had never thought possible before. Here was this humble individual, fully accepting that they themselves were insignificant, that their journey with God had not felt tangible, much less remarkable, at the time. Nevertheless, on reflection, the most beautiful story of walking with God had become visible. It is unavoidable to hear the testimony of this life and not see the hand of God, even in the brokenness and pain, maybe even more so. Consequently, I can only hope that when I reach that moment where I turn around and reflect on my own journey, that I too am faced with the unavoidable truth that God himself walked with me too. In the same way, I hope that this book inspires a similar reflection in those who read it, and in that I acknowledge that God must have His own design and purpose for the writing of this book, far beyond our mere storytelling.

Beckie Welch

I am immensely grateful and thankful to Beckie for crafting this biography with such grace and insight. Her writing of the story of Living Springs with the interweaving of many individual stories, including that of Jane and myself has been an exciting and at times a very intimate journey. I am profoundly grateful to her for guiding every step. Her thoughtful prose and tireless attention to detail have illuminated both the grand milestones and the quiet moments that define the journeys travelled by many. I thank all who have contributed in some way, which has helped Beckie to weave together memories, emotions and experiences into a narrative that feels honest, vibrant, and unique.

Rob Chapman

CONTENTS

Throughout the book, pseudonyms have been used to protect the identity of families who received support through Living Springs.

PROLOGUE

One summer's day, a young couple were walking through local woodland when they became aware of the presence of a gentleman. As they walked, he casually began to walk in step beside them, while making conversation. The gentleman was upright in stature with a kindly, engaging face and very softly spoken. Whilst they were talking, they noticed that attached to his belt was a unique-looking pouch. As though aware that the pouch had become the focus of their attention, he reached down into it, pulling out a collection of seeds. The couple marvelled at the colours and intricacies of those he held tenderly in the palm of his hand. Silently, they watched as he knowingly examined each individual seed, as though he was searching for one in particular. Upon its identification, the seed was carefully selected and placed gently into the couple's hands. In awe, they stood and held the precious seed together without a whisper, the wind blowing through the gently swaying trees, sending a small shiver through their bodies; their minds full of questions. But when they looked up, the gentleman was no longer present.

On arriving home, the couple chose a much-loved place in their garden, where the sun's dappled light seemed to dance across the earth. It seemed natural that they should treat the seed with the same tenderness, so they buried it there in the warm soil, lovingly watering it every day, and watching over it in anticipation.

As time passed, the seed became a tree which grew magnificent in its beauty. Regardless of the season, the splendour of that tree was undiminished; even in winter, as its leaves drifted to the ground, it seemed to stand majestic in its place. It became a place of refuge, not only for the couple, but for those from neighbouring villages. Whether to rest in the shade from the heat of the sun or shelter from the passing rain, it became a place of safety and beauty. Similarly, the animals, who made their homes around the tree, found shelter in its branches, while the birds nested in the sturdy branches, and the woodland creatures burrowed down into the safety of its sturdy roots.

Unnoticed at first however, ivy began to grow, winding its way around the trunk. Little by little it grew, its long green fingers reaching higher, until it enclosed the whole tree, shrouding its shape and diminishing its beauty. It covered the tree so completely that it could not be distinguished from all of the other trees. Its splendour disappeared from sight, as did the people who once treasured the place of refuge.

The stories of this great tree were passed down to the next generation, arousing interest in its former glory. As more of the villagers recounted the splendour they had once beheld, they desired to see for themselves and set about removing the ivy, steadily unwinding its grip. On uncovering the tree, they saw evidence of where branches had been broken in earlier storms, yet the more they revealed, the more amazed they became. Where the early branches were broken, they were smattered with new growth.

The couple were astounded at the recovery they saw before them, and word spread through the surrounding villages. It didn't take long before people were again seeking refuge beneath the tree, marvelling at the peace and beauty they beheld. The couple were now aware of the care needed to enable this beauty to remain, but they were also aware that their fading strength would not allow them to do this forever. And so they remained, like watchmen, vigilant to the arrival of another to take their place.

(A God-given vision written by Rob Chapman: 2018)

INTRODUCTION

This is the story of Living Springs, a charity constructed for the purpose of offering an alternative to mothers facing child loss due to abortion. This book follows the journey of the charity from its humble beginnings to the remarkable standing that it has achieved over time. Living Springs is often known for its incredible family-oriented work. Yet, few can retell the story of its origin.

Many charities are born from an individual's personal experiences, and this case is no different. In going back to the roots of Living Springs, the story of Rob and Jane Chapman becomes paramount. There are not many who are strangers to suffering, and yet some seem marked by a particularly heavy burden. For Rob and Jane, this came in the form of baby loss. Like most people, they viewed their future in simple terms: the desire for love, to raise a family and to find purpose in life. It is treated as a certainty, or even a felt right, and few people ponder the alternative. Yet, Rob and Jane soon painfully discovered that life is not always waiting to deliver those dreams.

Interweaving their personal journey is the experience of walking in faith with a loving God. It is a testimony of hope in pain, a light in darkness, and a representation of a life walked in companionship with Christ. This is the testimony of how God used the lives of Rob and Jane in their brokenness to shine a light of hope and healing for others, and in doing so, can demonstrate how God walks with us, if only we can surrender our lives to Him.

Earth has been tainted; it exists not in its full glory; it is shrouded in darkness. Yet it is in this darkness that glimpses of his glory can be seen most clearly, as in the darkness of the woods, the shafts of light shine down through the leaves, creating paths of glistening gold. In their silence they may go unnoticed, but to those who search diligently, they will be seen.

Chapter One

THE STORY OF THE SEED CARRIERS

- Rob Chapman and Jane Parrott -

- Rob's childhood -

Rob was born in 1946 in Old Hill, situated in the borough of Sandwell in the West Midlands. He was the youngest child of the family, having an older brother and sister (Arthur and Mary). Prior to the birth of Rob and his siblings, his father, Ewart, had established Chapman's Electrical in 1925. This business was to shape a large majority of Rob's life (the office space and shop for the business being attached to the family home). A significant portion of the family's time was devoted to the company, which naturally had a profound impact on Rob during his formative years.

In any family, a child will be influenced by each relationship, word, and action, giving an opportunity for a child to either be built up or knocked down, to feel loved and cherished, or alternatively, that they are a burden. No parenting fits neatly into one of these two categories, but unfortunately for Rob, his experience of childhood was tainted with difficulty: bullied while at school, he often heard harsh words and criticism, but the end of the school day did not mark an end to those challenges. His relationship with his father was distant, with Ewart dominating the family dynamic. He had a particularly argumentative nature (evident in work and at home), evoking anxiety within the family as to what may trigger an outburst. Over time, Rob developed the insight that this had affected his mother, Maud, who had become increasingly emotionally shut down. It is said that individuals can only give out of the love they have received. As time elapsed, Rob's mother simply did not have the resources to give, and Rob felt this loss too.

That is not to say that his early experiences were wholly undesirable. Rob fondly recalled attending a Christmas party in Birmingham with his parents and siblings at the 'Grand Hotel.' While travelling home, sleepy from the day's excitement, Rob snuggled up in his mother's arms, nestling inside her fur coat, which gave him genuine feelings of contentment and being tenderly cared for.

Thankfully, there was another individual in Rob's life who offered the kindness and gentleness that he needed. This person was Aunty Bitha (a name fondly used for Aunt Tabitha), a distant relation who lived with them through Rob's early years. Looking back, Rob would come to appreciate that if ever a seed was planted in his life for finding and experiencing the love of Jesus, it had been planted by her.

When Rob returned from school, Aunty Bitha would be sitting in front of the range, the warm glow from the fire behind her allowing her the light she needed as she sat to crochet or make rag rugs to add cosiness to the home. She gave comfort to Rob, who felt her loss keenly when she died in 1952, at 93 years of age. Although her death brought pain to Rob, he did not shed tears over her loss. Emotions were suppressed within the family, many issues went undiscussed and sharing feelings was not something that was encouraged or nurtured, partly due to the social norms of a post-war mentality, but more due to the relational difficulties within the family.

- Struggling to belong -

Rob continued to struggle in school, failing his Eleven Plus exam on his third and final attempt. Unfortunately, Rob was not aware at the time of being dyslexic (something which, had he known, would have explained some of the frustrations and disappointment he felt in his own abilities). Instead, his academic difficulties planted seeds of poor self-worth. Positively, more enjoyment and fulfilment were found during his time at technical school, where he studied physics, chemistry, engineering, drawing, and worked with wood and metal. As a child, Rob dreamed of being a policeman, yet the expectation was that he would join the family business, following in the footsteps of his two older siblings.

Throughout childhood, Rob demonstrated a keen commitment to pursuing his interests. He made his own money through a paper round and in desiring a new bike, he saved what he earned, slowly buying all of the parts he required and built it himself. Unfortunately, after treasuring the bike for many years, Rob returned home one day to discover that his father had given it away, which was a painful experience.

In his late teens, Rob became an independent character, his presence barely gracing family photographs, almost as though he were estranged from them. This was ingrained by his felt differences between himself and his family: an academically struggling boy with a flock of jet-black hair, in the midst of his more academically minded, red-haired siblings (a phenomenon that other family members themselves used to comment on). For Rob, this feeling of not belonging was so strong that he took a DNA test in much later years to eventually put the nagging thoughts aside. Although the test gave Rob the confirmation that he did belong genetically, emotionally he still struggled to find his place.

- *On the fringes* -

Rob was involved in numerous activities in the church of St Luke's: serving at the altar and in the choir and eventually teaching in the Sunday School, running youth clubs and serving on the Parochial Church Council. Yet for Rob, the church was not a place of belonging; he viewed these tasks simply as religious activities. In his mind religion was just another point of controversy, particularly within his family, illustrated when his father had taken him, embarrassingly, to confront the Vicar over some of the teaching that Rob had relayed at home. Frankly, Rob possessed no desire to pursue God more deeply and remained unaware of the true meaning of having a personal faith in Him.

At this point, Rob happily lived an independent life, relishing the confidence and control he felt in the direction he was headed. For him, this sense of self-sufficiency was perfectly illustrated in how he supported a work colleague, who had found that they were pregnant, but did not feel ready and able to have the child. They sought a solution in abortion, and Rob offered to provide financial support. At the time, he gave no thought to it, the role he had played, or indeed what he himself thought about the value of newly conceived life.

And so, this was largely how Rob spent his early adulthood - on the fringes of religion, searching for his own way. At that time, Rob was not receptive to new concepts or other evidences of truth, preferring to live in ignorance, not allowing his ideas to be challenged. Nonetheless, in those times seeds were planted and challenges lay dormant waiting for an opportunity to arise again. And as Rob entered early adulthood, his life began to reshape. The catalyst was a training holiday for those involved within the Sunday school ministry; it was here that he met Jane in 1967.

- Jane's childhood -

Jane was born in Hereford in December 1951, the third of four children, with two older brothers (Gordon and Ron) and a younger sister (Linda). When she was about five, the family moved to Tupsley, where Jane recalls happy memories of her time at Primary School. Due to growing up during a time when rationing was still in force, life was financially difficult for Jane's parents. However, by being efficient and mindful, they were always able to provide adequate food for the family.

Jane's parents operated within family roles that were normal in the fifties. Her mother, Joyce, was the bedrock of the home, being fully occupied with the cooking and cleaning which, at that time, meant hard physical labour: scrubbing the clothes and using a hand-operated mangle, sweeping the floors with a dustpan and brush, as well as meal preparation and baking from scratch.

Jane often asked her mother to come and play, but unfortunately, the responsibility of caring for the house and children left little opportunity for free time frivolities. Yet, Jane held vivid memories of the one-on-one moments that she did share with her mother. Jane's father had built a seat up in the branches of an apple tree in their garden. Jane's repeatedly frustrated efforts in trying to climb up to this haven were noticed by her mother, who appeared in the garden with the offer to show her how it was done. Her mother scurried up the tree identifying where the footholds could be found, closely followed by Jane herself. The moments of relaxed conversation that followed high up in the branches, surveying the landscape, were treasured by Jane. So much did she cherish uninterrupted time with her mother, she actually quite enjoyed the times that she was poorly because it secured her mother's time and attention: bringing hot soup and offering comforting cuddles.

Although Jane's mother did not have a lot of confidence in herself, she proved herself to be kind and gentle, as well as a talented woman (particularly when it came to baking). The birthday cakes she constructed in the form of treasure chests, ballet dancers and toadstool houses were a particular highlight. Her father even added electric lights to the toadstool house, so that it really was a wonder to behold. Another of Joyce's talents lay in needlework; she often sewed new dresses for Jane and Linda for their birthdays. Jane recalled her mother cutting up one of her own dresses in order to have the material she needed, highlighting the sacrifices she made in order to provide for the family.

Jane's father, Stanley, could also be described as a quiet individual, very studious and strict within the family. He seemed to possess the ability to appear instantaneously when the children were not doing what they ought to have been! Yet, he was also kind and generous, bringing the children home a chocolate bar each on a Friday after work. On occasion, you could also find the whole family in their parents' bed, enjoying a steaming cup of tea; something that also became a treasured Christmas morning tradition.

Stanley was a private man. In fact, when he was exploring faith, he did not share this with his family; instead, he started going out one evening a week, refusing to disclose his whereabouts. Eventually, when he was comfortable with his own decision, he announced to the family that he was to be confirmed, and from then on, he followed the Christian faith alongside his wife. Although Jane's father was quiet, he also had a sense of humour and enjoyed surprising the family with a trick or funny story. Particularly notorious was his famous 'cow trick': slowly dropping a pack of cards behind his back in order to create the perfect 'cow pat noise' as the cards slapped on the linoleum floor.

Jane's father was also hardworking, starting out as an office boy for the Hereford Times Newspaper and working his way up to managing director. This advancement also brought financial relief for the family, and Jane recalls the opportunity to participate in ballet lessons, which she relished. This job also enabled Stanley to afford a caravan holiday each year in Croyde Bay for his family, creating many wonderful memories for Jane: a daily treat of a fresh cream meringue, bodyboarding and fun with siblings, particularly Gordon, with whom she felt a strong affinity being rather similar in nature.

Although Jane experienced positive relationships with her parents, the same could not always be said for the relationship she had with her brother, Ron. It was not unusual for Jane to experience a significant amount of teasing and unkindness. The mocking imparted strong messages that she would not achieve anything or receive love from others, something which Jane would later acknowledge affected her self-esteem throughout her life.

- *The teenage years* -

Following a positive experience at primary school (and with a little extra support from the headteacher), Jane achieved the necessary grades to attend Ledbury Grammar School, based in a beautiful mansion house, with only three hundred students. She relished the opportunities she had there, particularly with her involvement in sports and dance, which she enjoyed more than academic subjects. Unfortunately, Jane did not get to complete her studies at this school due to a change in family circumstance.

The hard work and devotion that would later be evident in Jane could be identified in her father. Remarkably, her father achieved his Open University degree at age sixty-one, and was only stopped from achieving his honours course in 'Numerical Computation', when he sadly lost his eyesight to diabetes.

Jane attended a Church of England (C of E) church alongside her mother and, at the age of thirteen, made the decision herself to be confirmed. Fully believing that this was a turning point in her life where she would no longer sin, she was distraught to find that on the very afternoon of her confirmation, she argued with Ron. Feeling disheartened, she shared with God her disappointment in her 'failed confirmation' and acknowledged she had absolutely no understanding of how to 'manage to be good'. On completing school, Jane became more widely involved in her local C of E church: participating in Sunday School teaching, altar serving, bellringing with her sister Linda, as well as pastoral visits (something she thoroughly enjoyed).

- The happy couple -

During the next five years after they had met on the Sunday School training holiday, Rob and Jane dated. As Jane was five years younger and therefore still studying, Rob would pick her up at the end of the school day in his car, creating quite an impression on the other students! Over the following years, Rob and Jane both worked: Rob at Chapman's Electrical and Jane at Sainsbury's. They began to consider their future more seriously, and when they weren't together Rob could be found at

Fern Cottage: the derelict property they had bought and were renovating as a family home. After a five-year courtship Rob and Jane married on May 28th 1973, and moved into Fern Cottage together.

Rob and Jane enjoyed their time together as a newly married couple. They began to work together in the family business. For some this level of involvement may have been too overwhelming, but they felt comfortable and it didn't take long before they were finishing each other's sentences. They respected one another deeply and enjoyed the mutual company and care that they shared, setting a strong foundation for the journey ahead.

Although Jane had previously undertaken specific roles in church, unbeknown to her she too had still to develop her understanding of a personal faith in Jesus. She was therefore rather offended when a good friend, Val, handed over a pamphlet entitled 'Becoming a Christian'. Feeling disgruntled at this apparent oversight in her religious experience, Jane tucked the pamphlet away on the bookshelf without a second thought.

It was only sometime later (in 1977) when Jane sat alone one evening that the pamphlet caught her attention. Through reading the information, she gained a new understanding of what having a personal relationship with Jesus meant. On re-reading it the following morning, Jane decided to pray the response prayer on the back of the leaflet, which without any trumpet blasts or angelic presence, marked the beginning of real change in Jane's life and a lifelong faith journey. Finally, Jane understood the true essence of the gospel - man has been freely given that which they do not deserve: it cannot be earned through good works... it is a gift of love.

At this point, Rob had drifted away from his church commitments. He felt dubious about the authenticity of the joy that seemed to be displayed in church, which left him feeling frustrated. This was reinforced by his experiences with some individuals he knew were church attendees: people who professed one thing with their lips, but whose actions fell far short of their testimony. Perhaps, these experiences hooked into his already damaged view of hypocritical Christianity from his childhood. As a child, he had stood in church watching someone he knew well taking around the offering bag, someone considered 'an upstanding member of the community', and yet, the life outside of church resembled that of an entirely different man.

It was all too easy for Rob to justify his own behaviours and choices that kept him away from church and accept his own shortcomings through the use of comparison: 'Well, at least I am not like that.' Rob recalled playing golf with two genuine Christian men, amply displaying the love of God. And yet whose testimony was ignorantly dismissed simply because it didn't fit the narrative that Rob was living by. Because of these differences, faith was not something that Rob and Jane shared in much depth as a married couple. Rob developed the opinion that they both had their own individual pursuits; he had his love of cricket, and Jane had her newfound love of Jesus.

Chapter Two

THE JOURNEY TO THE WOODLAND

- experiences of loss -

Four years into their marriage in 1977, Rob and Jane began to try for a family. Over the next ten years, they experienced a heartbreaking amount of loss in the form of miscarriage. It was towards the end of 1978 when Jane first fell pregnant. Jane successfully carried the baby for the first six months, but devastatingly in May 1979, Rob and Jane experienced loss for the first time. During her stay in the hospital, Jane was placed in a bed alongside a woman who was recovering following her second abortion. For Rob and Jane, this provoked a cacophony of thoughts and feelings as they sought to understand the circumstances that had led the individual to give away the opportunity that they longed for so deeply.

It was in this moment that Rob and Jane saw a glimmer of opportunity to walk alongside others. Knowing personally the pain of their baby loss, they could feel keenly the grief that others may experience in situations where they felt they had no other alternative but to abort. They were both victims of baby loss, both experiencing emotional pain and grief. But where Rob and Jane were helpless in their baby losses, they began to understand that for some women, a need for support existed that would offer them an alternative to abortion.

It was during this time that Rob suffered another bereavement, the loss of his father, who died in 1980. This left Rob with many unprocessed emotions around their complex relationship. It settled in a tangible feeling during the funeral of not having really 'known' his father. This is probably not an uncommon scenario for those who lived during that time. That generation of men led a difficult life, employed in dangerous and difficult work down the mines, or away fighting in wars. Many did not ever come to terms with their own trauma, and lived a life emotionally shut down. Having not shared his inner world with his family, it left a void of not knowing who the man really was, including what sentiments he held towards his family. Regrettably, this dynamic tended to inadvertently impact the following generation who similarly did not fully understand how to share their own emotions with others. So it was that Rob recognised his lack of connection with his own emotions, let alone the knowledge of how to communicate them to others, both of which influenced the way he responded to the baby loss he experienced.

Rob and Jane still desperately wanted a family of their own and were excited to find out they were expecting again. However, in September 1981, they also lost this baby at three months gestation. Unfortunately, this occurred while Rob was out at cricket. When arriving home after his post-match drinking session, Rob was met by a heartbroken Jane, who told him of the miscarriage. They both felt the loss of not being together in that moment to comfort each other, and Rob would later regret his choices and the impact this had on Jane.

Jane fell pregnant a third time and, holding on to every hope, progressed to six months gestation. However, it was evident that something was not right; experiencing a high level of pain, Jane was admitted to hospital. They found that sadly the baby had died and Jane's body was trying to expel the baby. The delivery room was crowded with doctors, nurses and medical students. Jane then bravely underwent the distressing delivery, with Rob devotedly by her side. Rob watched as the baby entered the world. Aghast by the sight of their perfectly formed baby boy, lifeless and grey, being carried away. The image imprinted on his mind, never to be forgotten. It was a sight so heart-wrenching that one of the trainee doctors could not stay in the room. There was a tangible silence and pain in that moment that seemed to be felt by all those present.

In 1982, Jane fell pregnant a fourth time. Considering the history of loss, they were anxious, hoping against hope that this pregnancy would make it successfully to term. Yet, agonisingly, history was to repeat itself and in June 1982, they had to deal with another loss at three months gestation.

Although present physically for this miscarriage, Rob reflects that he did not give enough emotional support to Jane. At that time, emotional and mental support was rarely talked about - the journey of baby loss was one travelled alone. No follow-up appointments took place after the losses, and so the emotions were tucked away, even between husband and wife. Without guidance as to how to discuss and experience strong emotions Rob and Jane pushed them down, using physical sports to release what they felt, letting life carry on as though nothing had taken place.

This phenomenon of not engaging emotionally with baby loss was not something that existed only for Rob and Jane, but it was generally how parents were treated. In the hospital, procedures were of a purely clinical basis, with the baby being taken away as a waste product. There was no support or recognition given to the need to grieve such a loss. It seemed to be assumed that these bereaved parents would leave the hospital and fall back into daily life. But of course, most individuals cannot experience such loss and not be deeply impacted. Emotions suppressed will find their outlet somewhere and eventually impact a person in one way or another.

- Searching for hope -

The loss of four children left the desire for a family repeatedly slipping out of reach, and the possibility of ever having children increasingly unimaginable. So Rob and Jane began to look into adoption. During 1982 and 1983, they wrote at least thirty letters to various agencies and social services across the country in the hope of beginning the process. Throughout those two years they received a smattering of replies, the same words catching their attention repeatedly: 'sorry, unlikely, not suitable'. Eventually, they acknowledged that they had exhausted another avenue of hope.

Many people experience hardships, and it can lead them to become bitter and angry. But for Rob and Jane, it seemed to develop a level of humility and resilience. For Jane, it led to reflection on the purpose of life itself, and she learnt to depend on the hope that can be found in trusting in God. She experienced the reality of the words found in Romans 5:4 - suffering produces perseverance; perseverance, character; and character, hope.

A few months later, Rob and Jane came into contact with a specialist who thought there would be hope of Jane being able to carry a baby to term. They bravely agreed together to put their trust in the specialist, in the hope that this could lead to the fulfilment of their wish for a family. It was a difficult and invasive procedure of placing a stitch around the cervix to prevent preterm birth. An intervention that also required Jane to spend three months in hospital prior to the due date. The whole process was an intense waiting game. So much so that during that time, Jane expressed that whatever the outcome, she could not entertain the thought of going through the process again. Rob agreed. Whatever the outcome of this pregnancy, this was to be the final step and so whilst Jane was in hospital, Rob underwent a vasectomy. Now every conceivable hope lay in the current pregnancy.

Thankfully, there was cause for celebration. Following news from the hospital, Rob drove from Bewdley to Birmingham, full of anxious anticipation. On arrival in the delivery suite he sat, Jane's hand in his, as she summoned all the effort she needed for this moment. On June 8th 1984, Jane and Rob finally became parents to a wonderful baby boy, whom they named Peter. Elation filled their hearts and, in that instant, they felt an overwhelming relief at having seen their child delivered safely into their hands. For that moment, Rob and Jane were separated from the grief that they had felt over so many years as they beheld their beautiful dark-haired baby.

For hours, Jane lay snuggled up with her precious newborn, staring into the eyes of the one who had finally made her a mother. Rob drove home, marvelling at the miracle of new life. Unsure of what to do next, he stood in the garden watching the most beautiful sunrise he had ever seen: bright rays, hues of orange and gold glinting in the reflection of the windows, clouds wrapped in warm pink haze. Awe and wonder filled his heart as he paced the garden whilst the sun climbed higher in the sky.

- *Finally parents* -

It would be tempting to paint the following months as pure bliss, but that is not the reality of life. The next six months were hard work: Peter did nothing but cry. The only time he wasn't distressed was when he was pushed in the pushchair or driven around in the car, until these became stationary and then the crying continued. Life as a new parent was tough. Peter was an eagerly awaited blessing, but it was not easy. Thankfully, he eventually started to settle and became a cheerful, placid little infant. Yet, even then life is fragile. When Peter was around six months old, he fell sick with an extremely high temperature. He was admitted to hospital, but the doctors could find no apparent reason for his sickness and were highly concerned for his survival.

As Jane sat in the hospital, holding the hand of the most precious gift she had been given, she was reminded of the call Abraham received to sacrifice his son (the son God had given to fulfil a promise to create a great nation through him). Up until now, Jane viewed that story as an allegory of trust, but in that moment, she realised that life had led her to the same choice: to surrender all to Him and trust Him fully in acknowledgement that He is ultimately in control. She prayed, recognising that although she had desired Peter so much, if God wanted to take him, he could. The next morning, Peter regained his health, much to the amazement of the medical team who were unable to offer any explanation of what had occurred, either in sickness or recovery. Peter left the hospital in full health, but Jane also left with a renewed heart, having known something of full surrender to God.

For the remainder of his early childhood, Peter was a happy, healthy and contented little boy. Enjoying the safety and care he felt in the routine that his parents had provided for him, he was able to flourish. On the whole, there were no battles for bedtime; in fact, Peter often identified when he was ready for bed, asking his parents to come and tuck him in. He awoke pleasantly in the mornings, having a little chatter and play to himself, allowing his parents time to wake up gently. He endearingly established such a regular routine within the family that Rob and Jane relied upon this and chose not to set an alarm in the mornings. They reflected with great humour, how during a week of no particular plans and places to be, Peter had slept in on the only day they had planned to get up and go to church: Christmas morning!

As wonderful as raising her young boy was, as time passed Jane felt the grief of not being able to have another child. In December 1985, she expressed her frustrations towards God, feeling how unfair life can seem when individuals who would make wonderful parents can be those who experience difficulty in conceiving a child. In this struggle, she was reminded that God does not promise to take away the pain and suffering or to give all that is desired. But in hearing desperate cries, He remains close (Psalm 34:18).

That evening Jane had a dream, imagining herself in a big house, working with mothers and their babies. The next morning, she recalled this as no more than a strange dream and the day continued as normal. And yet she was unable to forget what she had visualised and grew to believe that God had given it to her as a calling. She began to pray into what she had seen, trusting God to intervene with her husband who was not yet a Christian, speculating that he would struggle to understand her conviction that she had been called by God. After several months Jane ventured the idea to Rob: that she desired to sell the house, buy a larger property and invite mothers and babies to live alongside them.

Having himself suffered the pain of miscarriage, Rob's heart was already primed in his compassion towards pregnant young women to offer an alternative to abortion. And so, on hearing what Jane felt called to do, he wholeheartedly supported the idea. Naturally, the driving forces behind their decisions were different: Jane had felt called by God, and Rob was enthused by his humanitarian instincts to offer support for an identified need. Yet, their drive and purpose were united in the pursuit of what they were to undertake together. It was the combination of these motivations which produced a strong blend of practical skills, determination and faith in God.

Chapter Three

THE SEED BEGINS TO GROW

- putting the vision into action -

Rob and Jane began to discuss what this vision would look like in practical terms. As they researched, it became clear that the idea was not financially viable. The property needed to be significantly larger than their current home, and consequently would require a lot of extra finance. For Jane, following this dream would be to walk a path that was littered with unfavourable conditions, meaning she would learn to trust God more deeply. Relying on his own business skills, alongside his practical expertise with properties Rob was not deterred either, and so they persevered.

With this determination, they searched up and down the country in order to locate a suitable property. They travelled sometimes many miles to view a property, only to realise that it wasn't what they wanted. Although disappointing, they weren't wasted journeys: the more properties they saw, the more they clarified what they needed to suit their purposes.

That being said, even after identifying ideal properties, they found that they were always out of reach for them. As well as the financial issues, the opportunities to pursue any of these buildings were quickly snatched away from them. During that time there were a group of property developers specifically searching for old barns and agricultural properties to renovate and sell as individual homes. Naturally, they had a much larger budget, so could easily outbid any amount that Rob and Jane could offer.

Rob and Jane at last discovered 'Enville Rectory', a stunning property being sold by auction, with a beautiful curved staircase and intricate handrail that wound down to the hallway. The excitement was tangible: this could be it. They assessed their finances and consulted a friend in the building trade to learn the costs of altering the property in order to make some part of it liveable. Rob and Jane were anxious with excitement, viewing this as the backdrop for the vision they held.

On arriving at 'The Cat' in Enville (where the auction was to take place), Rob and Jane stood at the back of a crowded room, full of anticipation. They experienced quite a shock when they heard the opening bid had far exceeded their maximum budget. They completed the auction on the pretence that they had already realised the property was not what they were looking for, and therefore were opting out. Although this was a huge disappointment, it had given a benchmark for the type of building they were seeking.

Rob and Jane do not romanticise the reality of chasing their vision. It was not a daily experience of signs and wonders. In fact, it was a journey that more closely resembled some of the more challenging stories in the Bible. Joseph spent thirteen years as a slave and a prisoner before God fulfilled his dreams, Abraham waited twenty-four years to gain the son he was promised, and Moses spent forty years in the desert before being called to Egypt. And in a similar way, Rob and Jane continued over the next two years with this process of trying to locate a property: searching, travelling, missing out.

Eventually, a property was put on the market called 'Barratts Coppice Farmhouse' in Stourton. The location was a huge advantage, being situated in easy travelling distance to Rob's work. It seemed ideal. So, when Rob and Jane arrived to view the property, they were understandably disappointed on recognising one of the notorious property developers. Seeing him at the house Rob felt his heart sink, as he muttered under his breath, 'Not you again!' Miraculously though, Rob and Jane were not in competition for this building due to it having tenants in its outbuildings. Interestingly, what was seen as a complication for the property developer became a blessing for the couple, removing competition and giving them the opportunity to buy the property.

- Finding the finances -

In that moment, a glimmer of hope began to grow. It was time to seriously examine how this dream could be turned into a reality. The cost of the property alone far exceeded the value of the family home they would be moving out of. In terms of even being able to borrow enough money, there were significant difficulties. The maximum mortgage that Rob would have been allowed to take was nearly quadruple their current mortgage, which consequently came with huge repayments that they had no possibility of making. They had no alternative but to dismiss this as an option. Still believing that the vision was worth pursuing, they began to examine every bit of available finance they could allocate to the property.

Rob and Jane's commitment to pursuing this path could be described as risky, some would undoubtably say irresponsible and admittedly it was incredibly difficult. But maybe that's the point: to not be able to create a backup plan and to rely solely on God's provision. It is a common reaction that as soon as things become difficult or fail to make sense within societal norms, people start wondering...maybe this wasn't God's plan after all. However, there are numerous stories in the Bible that counter that argument: Joseph was imprisoned and despised for his dreams, Moses struggled to lead the chosen people to the promised land. It often costs to be countercultural and do God's will.

Thankfully, Rob and Jane came across others who understood this. In hearing about their vision to open up their family home, a close friend offered his support. He approached Rob and Jane with an offer of a personal loan for the remainder of the property value, to be repaid over five years. So, with the combination of the equity from their current family home, the mortgage in principle and the personal loan, the purchasing of this property became a possibility.

- *A trail of complications* -

Soon after agreeing to the purchase, Rob and Jane received the news that the owners of the property, Marsh Trust, had included a covenant within the sale conditions of the property. This covenant was in place to ensure that no alterations or building work could take place without their explicit permission. The solicitor advising them recommended that they sign the covenant, for fear that they would lose the property if they refused. After such a long search, Rob and Jane were certainly tempted to sign to hold on to the property, but they stood firm and refused, aware that it could compromise the fulfilment of their dream. A few days later, all involved were surprised and relieved to find that Marsh Trust had made the decision to remove all covenants entirely, leaving them free to purchase the property and subsequently do as they wish.

Regrettably, not long after celebrating this victory, there was another issue, this time with the sale of their own family home. On discovering that the neighbour had a covenant in place to forbid building work near the perimeter of the house, the buyer threatened to pull out of the sale (as his desire for the home was to renovate the garage into office space). At the thought of having to fund two mortgages, Rob and Jane spent a few stressful weeks negotiating, eventually having no alternative but to pay the previous neighbour to remove the covenant, a payment that was unbudgeted for and a stretch for the already tight finances.

Finally all was settled, and on the 30th December 1986 Jane and Rob moved into the Farmhouse with their eighteen-month-old son, Peter. This was the first step in being able to embody their dream. Situated in a rural setting, this property had the potential to become a place of peace and tranquillity, nestled in the middle of rolling countryside and farmland, although in that moment it required significant imagination to visualise the beautiful, rustic house that it was to become. In reality the evidence of disrepair was unavoidable: the roof leaked (in fact on some of the buildings around the courtyard there was no roof at all), the building hadn't been cared for properly in a long while causing it to lose all of its personality and former charm and there wasn't even a path or defined entrance to the property.

- An uncomfortable beginning -

Rob and Jane certainly experienced their fair share of challenges once they had moved in. The winter of 1987 was particularly harsh, with freezing temperatures and a wind chill factor of minus 17 degrees. With no heating, aside from four open fires, they would wake up to scrape the ice from the inside of the bedroom windows. They often reflected with humour that their rugs resembled magic carpets as they rippled with the wind that blew under the floorboards. The standard of living could be described as anything other than comfortable.

To rectify some of the discomfort, they undertook the installation of central heating in the property, which was a huge task in itself, aside from the fact that a new gas main had to be dug one hundred and fifty metres across the field. Coincidentally, Rob knew someone who had access to a digger and was willing to complete this work for a reduced rate. As an added bonus, he also dug out a pool, which would later become the home to ducks and other wonderful wildlife. Once this task of digging was completed, Rob focused on getting all the plumbing in the house done, working on the evenings and weekends around his job.

At times it seemed overwhelming, and for many it would have been, but Rob was able to rely on his experience of having already renovated two properties. With this experience and the organisational skills that his father had imparted to him as a young adult, Rob had quite a skillset to depend on. There were nevertheless many days of hard labour, without the pleasure of a nice warm soak at the end of the day: just a rusty, leaking bath which they had had to attempt to plug with a cloth so they could wash before all the water drained away.

Frustratingly, not all the jobs seemed to be moving the renovation forward. After a particularly heavy rainfall, the fields behind the property had flooded. The surplus water ran down, flooding into the house. The only option was to knock a hole into the wall on the opposite side to allow the water to drain away again; a job that would later need rectifying, as well as work to ensure that the house would not flood in the same way again.

Not only were the physical living conditions difficult, but the finances also became unstable due to mortgage interest rates rising to nearly 15%. This not only affected their personal financial position, but that of the business too, with the family struggling to keep it viable. Paying the mortgage and buying essentials was a persistent worry, which caused them to ration money for food and sell items to make ends meet, cashing in life policies and selling the personalised number plate as well as inherited family possessions which they treasured.

- *Walking with God* -

The difficulties gave Jane a chance to understand the significance of trusting God in the face of adversity (being hard pressed, but not crushed, perplexed, but not in despair; all because of knowing the incredible power of God - 2 Corinthians 4:7-8).

In that way, it was during this difficult financial season that the presence of God was felt so tangibly. On numerous occasions, there was evidence of God's closeness and compassion in the minutest of details. On one occasion, a close friend of Jane had sadly been in a car accident. Jane wanted to send her some flowers to share her love for her, yet their budget simply did not allow it and she had to accept that the spend would be unjustifiable. She took her desires to God, laying out her heart in prayer. Shortly after, she received a call from a friend explaining that she had been gifted a bouquet of flowers, but they would be wasted as she was leaving for a holiday the following day, and so she wondered if Jane would be able to make use of them. Jane was touched by this miracle. She had been able to fulfil her desires of caring for another person in their time of need and felt that this was an expression of God's heart for the way life should be lived... a life spent loving others.

Life was often difficult for Rob and Jane. Most days consisted of putting one foot in front of the other, simply trusting and hoping they were walking in the right direction. The future was often uncertain, but along the way Jane's faith was strengthened by glimpses of God's loving hand at work even in the seemingly insignificant. It was in the vein of caring for others that again she experienced a real moment of God's blessing. Rob had kindly invited a couple of friends to dinner, against the backdrop of barely being able to put enough food on the table to feed themselves. Jane managed to source the majority of what they needed, but did not have the potatoes to complete the meal. Having no money to purchase any additional food, Jane acknowledged that she had done all she could and offered her circumstances to God.

Later in the day, Jane was asked by a friend, a local farmer, if she could take care of their two children while they took their other child to a presentation. Jane eagerly agreed, enjoying the busyness and laughter of having children around. When the farmer and his wife returned to collect the children, they stated they had got something in the back of the truck that they wanted to leave with them. As the farmer opened the doors of his truck, he revealed a sack of potatoes. It was the most exciting bag of produce Jane had ever received and another overwhelming reminder of the provision and closeness of God. The farmer was somewhat surprised as he received an emotional exclamation and a hug!

- *The developing property* -

Gradually, repairs were made to the house (huge projects for a couple of hardworking parents). Draft excluders were added to every sash window to try and keep in the warmth. Two bathrooms were installed, one for the family and the other for the guests. Rooms were divided or walls knocked down to create the ideal floor plan, and new plasterboard was installed throughout. The renovation took significant vision, none more so than the pigsty which was to be converted into the kitchen. The brick wall had to be cut through in order to install windows, a task that led to one of the instances that Rob would later reflect on as a demonstration of God's hand in their lives. Cutting in the windows was a heavy job and as Rob tore through the brick with a petrol diamond twelve-inch disc cutter he slipped, the spinning blade ripping through his trouser leg. He was unscathed but taken aback by how close he came to a horrendous accident that could have easily resulted in the loss of a limb, but besides a few frayed threads, he was unharmed and the work could resume. The pigsty soon became an extension of the main house and was transformed into a fully equipped kitchen.

Recognising that the house was becoming more manageable, Rob and Jane began to contemplate forming a charity, which of course, led them to wonder what the charity should be called. In line with how things had developed up to this point, a plan seemed to unravel before them: ideas emerged as they went about their daily life. And so it was on a cool, sunny day when Rob sat weeding in the garden, enjoying the warmth of the sun and the richness of the soil on his hands, that the words 'Living Springs' dropped into his mind. He shared this thought with Jane, and they both felt that there was something about these words that resonated with them. In some way they encapsulated what they felt they wanted their home to be.

As each part of the house was completed, another job naturally took precedence for the following few months: as the inside of the house became more presentable, the focus shifted to the outside and the idea of a walled garden seemed most fitting. As ever, finances were an issue. The bricks for the outside wall were budgeted for, but that left little to no budget for those they needed to border the garden. It came to their attention that Kendrick's corn store was being demolished and so Rob and Jane decided they would see if this could be used to their advantage. Having spoken to the site manager, Rob purchased the bricks for transportation costs. Much to their amazement a delivery arrived, in the form of two huge mounds of bricks, many broken, covered in mortar and rubble. During any free time for the following few months Jane was to be found perched amongst the rubble of thousands of bricks, painstakingly knocking mortar off each and every one, stacking them and making them suitable for use. There was something profound in the image of this work. In the dedication of rummaging in the dust of broken resources, lovingly finding what could be used to build this property into more of its likeness of the vision of God. She glimpsed something of what it is to be God's hands and feet: hidden in the background, labouring tirelessly.

Chapter Four

THE WINDS BLEW

- faith for the journey -

Over the following few years, a part of the house was refurbished to the point of having the first bedroom and bathroom suitable for expectant mothers. It was at this point that Rob and Jane were in a position to open up their home. They were aware that they would need support in allowing others to gain awareness of what they were offering. Jane had identified the charity 'CARE' (Christian Action, Research and Education) as the ideal platform to publicise to churches and other organisations across the country. Their input was too valuable an opportunity to pass by, with their work and ethos so much in line with what Rob and Jane were working towards.

And yet there was one staggering difficulty standing in the way of this possibility. There was a proviso involved in CARE being willing to offer their support: their expectation was that Rob and Jane must both be committed Christians. At this point, Rob would not have claimed that he was even on that journey. Undeterred by this glaringly obvious stumbling block, the application to join the 'Care Homes Programme' was submitted by Jane in August 1988, in the faith that God had given her a dream and he would bring it to fruition.

Following the submission of the application, Jane felt a burden to pray for the salvation of her husband with an urgency to do so both day and night for the following two months. In November 1988, the burden lifted, and Jane felt in faith that God had heard and answered her prayer. She felt sure that God had given her the date that she would see the results of her intercession (January 15th 1989). She shared this conviction with one other person, Adrian Watson, a trusted friend who had agreed to be a Founder Trustee for the future charity.

Unsurprisingly, the application to CARE was denied, and a meeting was arranged to explain this news to the couple on January 17th. Rob had so far been uninvolved in the application and was therefore unaware that they were about to be rejected on account of his beliefs. Jane still hoped that God had given her the date of Rob's conversion and that the situation would be turned around before the application was finally rejected. As the days passed, Jane waited in eager anticipation betwixt niggling doubts that she had imagined what she thought was this promise from God.

As a loving husband Rob encouraged Jane in her faith, but that was as far as it went. It was Jane's 'hobby' that he had little interest in picking up, and frankly he found the experience of being in church nothing more than irritating. The times Rob had attended church with Jane, he had left the meetings feeling angry and had further hardened his heart towards God. So, it was safe to say that the idea of Rob being converted at this point in his life was not very likely in terms of human rationality, but in spite of this, Jane held on to the belief that she had heard God speak and it was done.

- *Waiting on God* -

As the morning of the 15th January approached, Jane presumed that Rob would attend the Sunday morning service with her. However, at her request, Rob exclaimed, 'Why would I want to do that?' So it was that the morning meeting came and went, with only Jane and Peter attending, and the afternoon resumed with the usual work on the property. The job of that particular day was to dig out a trench under what had been the cattle yard, in order to plant new hedging to border the property. Rob rode back and forth to the entrance of the property, transporting the concrete with a ride-on mower and trailer in preparation for building a bank to separate the property from the main road.

Still being convinced that Rob would come to faith in Jesus on this day, Jane committed herself to finding a way to enable Rob to come to church with her that evening. Repeatedly, the view of Rob riding away with a trailer full of concrete to be unloaded signalled an opportunity. Jane used each occasion to run inside and make phone calls to her friends, trying to secure a babysitter for the evening. By the late afternoon she had exhausted all the possibilities of her phone book, and with a sense of frustration, gave up her plans, alongside her hope that she had heard God correctly.

As the light faded an unexpected visitor appeared, Roger, a friend of both Rob and Jane. He explained to them that his usual evening service was cancelled to enable the congregation to attend Worcester Cathedral. He had decided that he did not wish to go with them and so had taken the opportunity to visit his friends. Jane felt a surge of hope that they had gained a potential babysitter, but was taken aback when Rob remarked that she had better get ready if they were to make it to church on time.

Rob and Jane were greeted at church by a lengthy worship session (similar to the worship session that had inspired Rob to leave in irritation partway through the service on the previous occasion he had been there). Throughout the worship session, Rob was surprised to find that his heart was thumping. The minister suddenly announced his belief that there were individuals present in the congregation who needed to come forward for prayer. Both Rob and Jane felt the conviction that this invite was for them, and yet both were reticent to go forward.

Jane was convinced that this was the point at which God would call Rob, but she did not want to push this herself. Unbeknown to her Rob was feeling overwhelmed by this experience, he muttered to God 'I will not move unless something happens'. At this moment Jane turned to Rob, sharing her belief that this call was for them, and so it was that Rob and

Jane stepped up to the front of the church where the minister proceeded to lead Rob in a prayer of salvation. Jane's sense of joy and thankfulness was immense: God had not only been faithful but had orchestrated every little detail that made this a possibility.

- Supported by a Christian charity -

The following Tuesday evening, Rob and Jane had expected the scheduled visit from CARE. However, eager to support Rob and Jane in their venture, the pastor of the church had already been in contact with CARE to enquire about the support that would be available to them both, and in doing so had mentioned Rob's conversion. Following this conversation, CARE delightedly shared the news that the application had been successful. Considering that only one in ten applications are accepted, it is remarkable that the bid was accepted with such rapidity and ease. Only after this conversation did the team at CARE reveal that they had felt convicted that this application was of God's doing, and as a consequence had spent time during their weekly team meeting praying for Rob's salvation.

In sensing that the vision for Living Springs was aligned with the vision they held for the CARE charity, they had fully committed their hearts to supporting Rob and Jane as they sought to offer their home to others. And although CARE was originally sought after in terms of what they could offer in promotion, they played a much more significant role. Rob and Jane were so thankful to the two founders of CARE, Charlie Colchester and Lyndon Bowring, for their input. They recognised the hard work that they dedicated to providing a financial gift, which allowed the work to begin, as well as outstanding emotional and practical support which allowed Rob and Jane to flourish.

- Pursuing faith as a family -

Faith became integral to the family's life: Rob, Jane and Peter attended church regularly. On Sunday, 18th June 1989, they attended a meeting which focused on Father's Day. During the children's work Peter was given the chance to discuss his father, and also spent time examining the importance of their Heavenly Father. As a result of this the children were given an opportunity to give their hearts to God, and Peter was one of those children who decided to do just that. Rob and Jane were filled with joy as Peter made this step in searching after God.

Over the following years Peter developed a personal understanding that the family lived in a way that God desired, and acknowledged the tangible presence of God. He came to hold his parents in high regard for what they had sacrificed, seeing the impact that it had on those that came to live with them. Not to mention that as a young boy he relished the space and opportunities he had to explore: riding his bike around the grounds, watching the mechanic in the outbuilding fixing up old cars and living alongside the farm.

- A personal journey of faith -

Although Rob had become a Christian, he struggled to see what that meant for him personally. A nagging feeling kept him questioning: 'What is different? What has changed? What impact has this had?' Having been repeatedly plagued by these thoughts, Rob arrived at the decision that he would be baptised. He thought that this might enable the conversion to feel more 'real', to give him some palpable experience and relationship with God and to begin a whole new journey. Rob had regularly heard the phrase 'ask and you will receive' (Matthew 7:7), and he had shared his desire to feel close to God many times. This left him to wonder whether the disconnection must be as a result of a specific sin or a lack of effort. If only more time was spent praying, if only the Bible was more well-read and understood. If only...

The baptism coincided with an incredibly difficult financial time: interest rates were again unstable, and Rob felt the pressure of making the monthly payments for both the house and business. All in all, this was a season of great difficulty and uncertainty for him, and so this was the backdrop for how he embarked on his journey into baptism, full of hope and longing to meet with Jesus in a whole new way, fully expectant to see some change materialise in his life.

The baptism itself had to take place in an alternative church location, due to their home church not having the facilities. The church service was underway and Rob eagerly waited for his moment. As he was introduced to the congregation as 'Rob Chapman, a very successful business man', Rob felt every hope and confidence drain away; he was not a successful business man, he was failing, and now he stood at the front of the church feeling a complete fraud. The pain was tangible. Rob underwent the baptism in body, but his mind was elsewhere. There was no feeling, and no lasting memory of the event; it became white noise in the background of his inner turmoil. He walked away from the waters of baptism in a more difficult emotional state than when he had entered them.

From this point onwards, Rob had to realign his understanding of what it meant to have a personal faith. If it was not some radical, life-changing moment (which he was aware it could be for some), then what did it actually mean for him to follow God? Simply put, Rob realised his commitment was to believe (Acts 16:31): a cognitive decision at its very roots which didn't discount emotional and spiritual experiences, but also did not elevate them. He reached the conclusion and gradually the acceptance that he believed in God, but for him this did not translate into a tangible feeling of God's presence. Instead, he committed himself to live in the way the Bible instructs: to act justly, to love mercy and to walk humbly with God (Micah 6:8).

It is with this in mind that Rob described his experience of God as more of a story of hindsight, where it was only on looking back that Rob saw where God walked beside him, guiding his steps. This resonated with the sentiments in the poem 'Footprints' written by Mary Stevenson, in response to questioning where God was in difficult times. Rob would hold on to and testify to the notion that when it seemed there was only one set of footprints journeying alone, it was then that God had carried him.

- Moments of change -

Aside from this struggle, there were definite moments where God's touch was evident in Rob's life. Not in the miraculous, but present in each life circumstance, nestled into the normality of the day, but enough to lead Rob to exclaim that he couldn't understand in what way certain events were possible: decisions were made that had once looked impossible, debts were paid from insufficient funds and there were moments of unexpected personal change.

One of these moments of personal change particularly resonated with Rob. From an early age, Rob had struggled with the concept of death due to teasing in his childhood. He was repeatedly poked in the sides and told to imagine that action as the worms eating his body in the ground once he had passed away. Understandably, this developed into fearful associations which inhibited his ability to discuss death. So, when nine months after his conversion, death was brought up in conversation, Rob immediately expected the sensation of fear to be triggered, and he inwardly prepared for emotional shutdown. But what followed was the realisation that his mind did not react as he anticipated: he was not fearful. The ties to that fear had been broken; there was no need to be fearful of death anymore.

Although Rob generally struggled to feel an emotional connection in his faith, he does recall moments where he felt God's gentle nudge one way or another. One of these particular stories related to a subtle reminder of Rob's vacillating opinions. Being in business with family could be so rewarding, albeit frustrating, with him and his brother, Arthur, having different opinions about where the business should be taken. Following one particular disagreement between the two brothers, Rob and Arthur both left the meeting grumbling, both aware that their difference of opinion was slowing down their progress. Naturally, thoughts popped up on how much easier it would be to work alone.

A year later, Arthur sadly suffered a heart attack; as a result, he began to increasingly withdraw from the company, with Rob taking on more responsibility over time. Many years later Rob found himself complaining again, but this time that Arthur had left all of the work up to him when he really needed a bit of support. The previous thoughts of it being easier to work alone came forcefully back to him, and he felt convicted that regardless of the situation he always found something to complain about. He felt God questioning: 'Isn't this what you wanted, to make your own decisions?' Although aware of his sinful nature, Rob also experienced the gentleness of God in response. More importantly, he gained a greater understanding of why God requires His people to depend on His will: without that firm foundation, believers are at the mercy of their own changing whims and emotions.

Through his journey to faith Rob has begun to connect more tangibly with his emotions. For the majority of his life he was unable to express his feelings, struggling to express emotion at the death of his mother and at the loss of their babies. This would have released some of the anguish, but the tears never came.

Over more recent years there had been a journey of emotional healing. As part of maintaining healthy spiritual habits, Rob attempted to make time to read and reflect on the Bible. As he sat one morning, he opened the Bible at the book of Luke and he began to read. On reading Luke 1:1, his eyes brimmed with tears. ('Many have undertaken to draw up an account of the things that have been fulfilled among us'). For Rob, this was one of the first moments of experiencing emotion. Taken aback, Rob questioned what the reason for it was. There was nothing particularly significant about the verse, yet it had triggered something. Out of curiosity Rob turned back to the same verse later that evening and found that he was reading those words through hazy, teared vision. Rob could not fathom why the verse had affected him emotionally, instead believing that in making efforts to move towards God, he had experienced the Holy Spirit opening up a part of him that was not previously accessible, and had since begun to lead him on a journey of emotional freedom and healing.

::: *Trusting God with finances* :::

Throughout the following year the financial situation again became unsteady; having nothing in the account other than what was necessary to pay the monthly wages. Rob worked tirelessly alongside other family members to keep the business going. As part of this, he visited the bank every day to deposit money and pick up the bank statement - he was living in perpetual fear. On walking back from the bank, statement in hand, he would peer in full of trepidation hoping that the business would still be able to pay the bills. He felt tremendous pressure, and it took its toll until he eventually reached breaking point.

On one particular day Rob struggled to even make it to the end of his working hours, and decided to go home at lunchtime to see Jane. Over lunch, he began to share the weight that he felt and the depths of his anxiety over the business, creating a rare opportunity for emotional vulnerability. As Jane sat and listened, she gently prompted Rob to give it to God: to surrender the pressure and to put the business in His hands. So together they prayed, laying it all down.

The following day Rob returned to the bank to pick up the statement. He was about to open the envelope when he felt a gentle prompting to trust. In that moment, he surrendered his need to be in ultimate control, placed the envelope in his pocket and headed back to work. He never again opened one of these statements feeling desperate to determine the safety of the business, and over the following years the company became more stable and profitable.

CHAPTER FIVE

A REFUGE AND RESTING PLACE

- learning from the first families -

With CARE's support, information was shared across local churches, identifying the Chapman home as a safe haven for those in difficult circumstances who found themselves pregnant. It offered an alternative for those who felt they had no other option but to abort their unborn babies - it was a lifeline. And so, as awareness of the charity grew, the families began to gather, and Rob and Jane filled the four spaces they had made available in their home.

It soon became evident that trying to distinguish between their own finances and those of the charity was overwhelmingly difficult. Trying to split the cost of a meal eaten together into the personal cost of their family and that of the guests was painstakingly time-consuming, not to mention that separating each and every penny did not lie in unification with the heart of the vision that had been placed within them. And so with that they decided that they would be self-funded, taking their first mothers in as 'guests' in their own home.

Rob and Jane understood the biblical expectation that in following God's will, the path will invariably lead to broken, suffering individuals. In Luke 5:31, Jesus highlights that it is those that are sick who require a physician and Jesus Himself would therefore choose to spend His time with the desperate and downcast. In fact, He continually demonstrated

His heart for serving others, and explicitly sets this as the example of how to live for those who love Him (John 13:15).

From the moment that Rob and Jane welcomed mothers into their home, they realised they had so much to learn. Rob recalled an incident that brought enlightenment to the role he had undertaken. On returning home one day, Rob cheerily greeted one of the mothers, Diane, who was sitting in the snug in front of the fire. She informed Rob that the coal had been delivered earlier in the day, leaving Rob somewhat perplexed owing to the fact that he hadn't ordered any. Diane adamantly explained to Rob that there had been a delivery and she herself had watched the driver carrying the sacks round to the back of the house. Feeling confounded Rob went off to investigate, only to find there was no sign of any coal at all. It was in that moment, staring at the empty space behind the house, that Rob realised the extent of the damage that these young mothers could be living with. He found that many lived in an element of their own fantasy world, generally, somewhere safe and predictable, something that did not always exist in reality. Both Rob and Jane learnt to live by the mantra... believe everything, but check all things.

- *Holistic care* -

Rob and Jane also grew to understand that their care and support were much more holistic than simply supporting mothers in finding an alternative to abortion. Through inviting these mothers into their home and their lives, they learnt what living life with others truly looked like and came to see how they could show love to these women, giving them value and importance. Through meeting Abeni, Rob and Jane felt the poignancy of how their care could impact the women individually.

Abeni had not spent long in England and was also growing up in a strict environment where pre-marital sex was forbidden, and therefore pregnancy would bring shame upon the family. So having found herself pregnant, she desperately searched for support, knowing that she did not want to abort this young life. It was agreed that Abeni could come and stay with them. So under another pretext, she moved out of her family home.

As the pregnancy advanced Rob and Jane spent much time caring for Abeni, and had developed a close relationship with her. One evening she shared her love of the traditional Christmas in England, the type you would find printed on Christmas cards. As it worked out, Abeni was still living with Rob and Jane over the Christmas period, and they therefore took her to attend a midnight mass at St Peter's, a 16th-century, picturesque church.

On that cold winter's night, they sat in the church as the choir boys entered, their candles flickered in the draught, and their angelic voices rose to the rafters as they proclaimed the birth of Jesus. The beautiful atmosphere made the hairs rise on the back of their arms and glancing over at Abeni, Rob and Jane could see that her eyes were glistening with wonder and awe as she beheld her dream becoming a reality... this was a lifetime's precious memory in the making.

Over the next few months, Rob and Jane supported Abeni as she approached the birth and the following adoption process. This was an understandably difficult time for any young mother, particularly without the presence of family support. Following the birth, Abeni returned home to her parents. However, overwhelmed by the emotions of the birth and the adoption that was to follow, she eventually confided in her mother. Wonderfully, her mother was supportive of her daughter and held her closely as she shared all that she had been through.

With this newfound support, Abeni made the decision to raise the child herself. They had known prior to this decision that the baby had been diagnosed with Down's syndrome and that raising them would therefore present additional challenges, but they embraced the challenge, desperate to rekindle the heart connection between mother and baby.

- Cherishing the small moments -

Rob and Jane had many opportunities to care for and love the babies residing in their home, as well as the mothers. Following the birth of two babies, Jane decided that the new mothers needed a little time to themselves, so she planned to take them out in the evening for a well-deserved treat. This meant that Rob had the job of caring for two precious little girls. As the young mothers and Jane emerged to say goodbye, they were greeted with the sight of Rob with the two babies snuggled up contentedly in his arms. Rob was in his element, gazing into their beautiful faces. This was the very core of what they had hoped to achieve: offering life where there was seemingly no hope.

It seemed to be in these moments, when they wanted to love and serve others, that God met them most profoundly. Jane would regularly take trips out with the mothers and babies. Understandably, this came with great difficulties considering that they owned a three-door car at the time: trying to manoeuvre the babies safely into the back of the car posed a significant challenge. Rob and Jane therefore assessed their finances agreeing to spend a portion of their savings. With this budget in mind, they visited Halesowen Motors, where they came across a Rover four-door car that looked ideal, disappointingly it was over the amount they had agreed between themselves. With some difficulty, they made the decision to use additional savings.

This became one of the stories that they, in retrospect, termed a 'loaves and fishes' event: for what occurred was unexplainable to them. Once they had purchased the car, they viewed their accounts, realising that they had not used any of the additional savings. The extra funds had not been there the evening before, and they could not locate a particular payment that had been paid in. There was just enough finance for the vehicle to be bought... it had been a gift from God.

So much of what was meaningful in the relationships with the mothers was found in the small moments, making memories for the families that they came into contact with, changing some of the landscape of their view and experiences of life. Jane worked closely with one particular family who had shared with her many of their life experiences. In these conversations, Jane found that the family had never been to the beach... not just the children but the parents too. As a result, a day trip was planned to Aberdovey. Regrettably, the whole journey took place amidst thunderous clouds and teeming rain. Jane felt so strongly that this family should have an enjoyable experience that she prayed fervently for a break in the weather. Following a very difficult journey, they made the turn into Aberdovey and Jane felt an enormous amount of relief and gratitude, and they were greeted by beautiful, clear skies. She relished the opportunity to observe the family playing and exploring the beach, viewing it as a privilege to have helped this family to create precious memories.

- A male role model -

Although the majority of the caring for the girls was done by Jane, Rob fell into a role of supporting the boyfriends who regularly featured in the lives of these mothers, but who did not live at the property. He would spend time sitting with them, befriending them, perhaps in some cases as the first positive male role model that they had experienced. The young men who found themselves in these situations were often equally as troubled as the mothers: experiencing poor finances, inadequate living conditions and poor emotional and mental health. Naturally, they too hungered for nurture and stability. Unfortunately, most of the support they needed was beyond the remit of the work that Rob and Jane had committed to, but they offered what they could.

One particular young man, Timothy, regularly sought out Rob's company, mostly when Rob was preoccupied with a maintenance job (he found that having an opportunity for someone to listen without having to be face-to-face created an occasion for moments of vulnerability). The majority of the time the conversation would be casual, allowing for companionship. But more importantly, this allowed trust to be established and when difficult issues arose, Rob would often be able to offer support.

Unfortunately, many of the situations were highly complex, with individuals facing numerous social and emotional issues. For Timothy, his circumstances proved to be overwhelming. Concerns were raised over his welfare, and Rob spent time trying to locate his home. On arriving, Rob realised that Timothy had planned to take an overdose. Thankfully, this was averted and although Rob could not change any of the circumstances Timothy faced, he could offer support and empathy. He could be there when Timothy would otherwise be alone, seeking to show that he was valued and loved.

- An altered perception -

Through the developing relationship with one mother, Lilianna, Rob recalled a moment of realisation that he was so unbelievably unaware of the depth of pain and suffering that many individuals live with on a daily basis. Over the time they spent together living as family, they had clearly formed a bond. One particular evening they sat in the snug, warming by the fire. As they shared the warmth, Lillianna began to share some of her life. As she watched the dancing flames in the fireplace, she recalled how her partner would force her to stand naked in the window, stripping her of all dignity... if she dared to move, he would burn her with his cigarette as a punishment. She shared details of how the majority of her beatings occurred in the bath. On seeing the perplexed faces, she explained that this was a place of no escape.

Rob was struck with the utmost realisation that he had held such a naïve and sheltered view of the world. Any remnant of the temptation to judge others for their actions was shattered. It was not uncommon for Rob and Jane to come across criticism for supporting these 'sluts' who had got themselves pregnant outside of marriage. And yet most of those who are tempted to pass judgement have not walked even a few steps in the agony that many of these mothers have spent their lives in. There is always a past, there is always a cause.

Looking back, Rob would highlight how essential it is as Christians to offer a way of hope. To comment on how individuals should live according to the Bible hinders the ability to share the love of God. It is easy to observe and comment on behaviours with a list of 'thou shalt nots', but it became Rob's conviction that what Jesus calls Christians to do is to demonstrate a way of hope, so at the very least, the choice to live differently is an option. That is what Rob and Jane sought to do: to offer an alternative based on Christian beliefs around abortion.

Rob and Jane tried to speak humbly of the role they had undertaken, not to be elevated above others or to claim a level of divine calling. They sought to embrace instead, however falteringly, the responsibility that each believer has to demonstrate love and to understand the practical out-workings of 1 Corinthians 13 4-7, *Love is patient and kind, it is not boastful or proud, it does not cause dishonour to others, it is not self-seeking...Love always protects, always trusts, always hopes and always perseveres.*

Chapter Six

THE TREE GREW MAGNIFICENT

- a developing charity -

Throughout the following couple of years, after Rob and Jane had moved into their new home the tenants moved on from the outbuildings they had rented, which fell in line with the timing of the redevelopment plans. With this in mind, Rob and Jane commissioned an architect to draw up some possible plans. Frustratingly, when they applied for planning permission they were firmly denied. As far as the council was concerned, it was a completely run-down barn of no historical value. Due to it being situated in the green belt, there was also the reticence to allow the building to be repurposed to anything other than its previous agricultural usage. Additionally, judgements about the centre itself and the type of women invited to stay further cemented the decision to disallow the renovation. Therefore, the planning permission was denied categorically (so much so that it was stated by one individual that the planning permission would be granted over his dead body). And so, an appeal was filed with the planning inspectorate based in London.

Many meetings followed with council members in the appeal to overturn the original decision. During this time, one of the individuals involved in denying the application had a niece who fell pregnant outside of marriage. This radically changed his thoughts and feelings about the work of Rob and Jane, so much so that he decided he wanted to support the work and voted in favour of the planning permission. As a well-thought-of man within the group, the vote swayed in the opposite direction, allowing the planning permission to be granted.

Yet, there was a caveat: planning had been granted on the condition of three criteria being met. One of which was the need to open out the entrance to the driveway to cope with the expected increase in volume of traffic to the property. This sounded relatively simple, but along the grass verge running parallel to the track stood a large tree that lay on council-owned land. Effectively, their planning permission had been denied: they had reached an impasse. But Jane, having been reminded of the Israelites crossing the Red Sea, was determined to take the matter to God in prayer. She fully trusted that God could make a way, believing that this was His plan and He would not let it be thwarted.

One evening, a very strange conversation ensued between husband and wife. On returning home from work Rob asked Jane about the disappearance of the tree, much to Jane's surprise who knew nothing of it. Even more alarmingly, a few days later Rob received a complaint from the council demanding to know why he had taken it upon himself to cut the tree down. Naturally, Rob denied all knowledge, explaining that he was unaware of what had happened. The council did not accept this version of events, and the phone call ended with a fairly robust threat of trouble if it was found that they had cut the tree down in order to gain the planning permission they had applied for. Following a few days of council investigations, it was found that the utilities company had identified the tree as interfering with the overhead cables. Having done so, it was perfectly in their rights to cut down the interfering tree, and that is what they had done.

This occasion serves as an example of the promise in Luke 17:6, which states that *faith as small as a mustard seed can move mountains.* The concept of moving mountains seems too abstract. And yet the story of the tree demonstrates God doing just that: rearranging part of his natural world on the basis of prayer and faith. In this, Rob and Jane were astounded at the power and sovereignty of God that had woven itself intrinsically through His plans for their lives.

- Reassurance -

In order to support Rob's developing faith, Rob and Jane attended a John Wimber Conference in September 1989. It was during this that they received confirmation that their work was in line with God's will. During the comfort break, Rob and Jane meandered across the hall in search of a coffee when they were approached by Pastor Rory. After general conversation they began to speak about the work they were doing from their home.

In a burst of excitement Rory interrupted them before they could expand any further, and proceeded to describe their home in great detail: converted barns that sat nestled around an open courtyard, a pigsty becoming a fully functioning kitchen and most importantly, gathered all around the property were families. The pastor could see it all; he had been holding on to this vision for some time, waiting for God to reveal who it was for. He added that he believed that the money to finance the work would come through refurbishing TVs (not dissimilar to what the family business, Chapman's Electrical, would later work on). This was a great comfort and affirmation - eighteen months after moving into the property, the vision was still being formed and revealed.

Financially however, it was still a difficult undertaking. Rob still felt the call to give regardless of the fact that they were already struggling. He was aware that making the decision to give a percentage of his money would push the already fragile finances more than would be wise. Nonetheless, he felt called to lay down his burdens and to trust: wholeheartedly trust that God was in control. Rob had already experienced the way in which God would meet them when they took a step towards Him, and so with a sense of peace that had not been present before, they placed the financial situation firmly in the hands of God. A bank account was opened where 10% of their earnings would be transferred to, alongside the declaration from Rob that he could not make his finances viable on account of this, and so was placing his trust in God that He would provide for them.

On this occasion they were trusting God as the lifeline, not as a backup plan. The culture they were living in was one of sharing that which was surplus to requirements. It was countercultural to live an uncomfortable lifestyle for the sake of others. Yet it is a way of living rooted in the Bible, an example of this is Zarephath, a widow and her son on the brink of death through starvation (1 Kings 17). It is to her that God sends Elijah to receive his sustenance. In doing so God was asking her to sacrifice everything, relying solely and faithfully on Him. Rob and Jane experienced the discomfort of laying down control of their finances, but in time they were to see how God was to provide for them, beyond their human reasoning.

- Before you call -

In the Bible, the psalmist speaks of the need to wait quietly before God, acknowledging that all hope is in Him (Psalm 62:5). In this way, prayer can be summarised as an active submission to God's divine plan. On occasion, there were miracles that Rob and Jane could not even have claimed to have prayed for.

When Rob returned home from work one day, he saw that there had been workmen resurfacing the road at the bottom of their drive. His eagle-eyed mind spotted an opportunity immediately. Just past where the men were working lay the bus stop that the mothers used on a regular basis. This bus stop could only be reached by trekking twenty yards over a muddy grass verge at the end of the drive, which considering that the majority of women were also pushing pushchairs, was far from ideal. Rob wondered whether there might be an opportunity to ask if they would consider creating a path in order to make it more suitable terrain.

Over the next few days Rob and the workmen became like ships in the night; he left for work before the workers arrived and arrived home after they had finished for the day. Frustratingly, as he drove towards the site on returning home from work one day, he noticed that the workmen had completed the job. Feeling a pang of disappointment that he had missed the opportunity to ask them to tarmac the verge, he indicated to turn into the property. As he slowed down, he glanced across and saw that the grass verge had been dug out and tarmacked, creating an easy route to the bus stop. It had not been requested, and there certainly had not been any advantage for the workmen in doing it. Rob gazed at it in amazement and uttered the words 'but why?'

- *Foster carers* -

Over time, Rob and Jane gained a good reputation through the work they had done with young mothers, so much so that they caught the attention of social services. In 1991, they were approached to see whether they would accept referrals for those who needed support within the social care system. However, with this request came the requirement for Rob and Jane to become foster carers. It was another challenging step, but it soon became clear that fostering was the right decision. Each request for foster care would vary depending on the individual's situation: sometimes fostering young girls with unborn babies, newborn babies or both the mother and the baby.

Positively, fostering brought in a fairly dependable level of income, which covered the costs of taking people into their home. As a consequence, Rob and Jane were released to use their own funds to continue the ongoing renovations. It also allowed Rob and Jane to offer support more widely, with fifty percent of the referrals now coming from outside the area.

On one particular occasion, Rob and Jane were asked to foster the baby of a mother with learning difficulties. They were essentially being asked to form a judgement on the capabilities of the parent. This added a whole new element to the work that they had previously been doing. As these situations arose more frequently questions were raised as to the basis on which Rob and Jane were qualified to form such judgments. Jane came to the conclusion that this was an accurate analysis of the situation and this prompted her to begin some formal training. In June 1997, she received her Diploma in Social Work.

Although fostering brought in new opportunities, it also created its own set of challenges. Taking mothers into their personal space had created a certain tension with Rob and Jane's own family and friends, as visiting them also meant visiting the mothers and babies. There was also the added complexity regarding the rules around fostering. Everyone who came into contact with the young mothers and babies had to be screened through the CRB (Criminal Records Bureau) process. For those reasons visitors became more of a rarity, and at times a sense of isolation was felt.

In spite of this difficulty Rob and Jane came to experience community in an entirely new way, with a steady stream of people who stepped into their lives to offer support and companionship. One such couple were Ruth and Alan Adams, who became close friends. Not only did they offer friendship, they also decided to become foster carers themselves, so that they could provide respite care in the house enabling Jane and Rob to be away from the house together.

- Dovetailed visions -

From the beginning, the heart of what Rob and Jane sought to provide was an alternative to abortion, but as their experience grew, they realised that there was scope for further support within the community. Acknowledging that their work was vitally important, they came to see that it would be beneficial to provide more holistic support and began to search for a way to make this a reality. As they looked back Rob and Jane both testify to how God had brought certain individuals along their path.

One of these individuals was Roger Eames. Jane had created a friendship with Roger when they attended the same church together in their twenties, and Roger had also formed a bond with Rob through playing golf. After a time of personal loss Roger came to spend a great deal of time with Rob and Jane, further cementing the relationship. Due to family circumstances, Roger found himself in the position of retiring early and viewed this as the ideal time to pursue his desire of opening a Christian centre, comprising of a coffee shop, counselling centre and bookshop. Naturally, as Rob, Jane, and Roger discussed their prospective visions it was evident that there was scope to bring the two together.

Jane, Rob and Roger travelled up and down the country and across the border into Wales to find the location that seemed to fit with this vision. After many disappointing trips they finally went to view a property right on their doorstop (on Stourbridge High Street). Seeing the potential of outreach from that property, Roger purchased it in 1990. As they were keen to work closely together, they pursued this venture under the auspices of the charity that was operating from Barratts Coppice Farmhouse.

So it was that in 1991 Roger opened 'The Well' coffee shop, shortly followed by the addition of a counselling centre above it. They came into contact with a renowned counselling professional, Roger Altman, who agreed to commute to Stourbridge to deliver training courses for people across the West Midlands for eighteen months (residing with Rob and Jane during the week). This built up a repertoire of individuals willing to support the vision for the counselling centre in Stourbridge. Rob and Jane completed the course themselves in preparation for opening the 'Pregnancy Advice Centre' which operated out of the counselling space. The idea was to offer a Christian-based service which supported people dealing with issues of promiscuity, low self-esteem and poor relationships. It also offered the perfect signpost for those who were searching for an alternative to abortion, but were struggling to find the residential support they needed.

At times it seemed that their visions clashed, but as Rob, Jane, and Roger journeyed together, it became clear that they were not in competition with each other, but their visions dovetailed in a way that supported and strengthened each of them and the services they were looking to provide. They recall a friend sharing that they believed Rob, Jane and Roger were like a three-strand cord: stronger together (Ecclesiastes 4:12).

As their outreach spread, Rob and Jane often wondered whether they were still pursuing what God wanted or if they had wandered from their initial vision. It was a great encouragement to receive a powerful affirmation through Roger Altman. During one of the evenings that they spent together, Roger shared a vision that he felt was from God, of Rob and Jane standing in front of a barn. He believed that God was saying

He would open the doors of the barn for them, allowing them to take whatever tools they wanted because He trusted them. It was a wonderful comfort and confirmation, knowing that they were in line with God's will and that He trusted them with what had been placed in their hands.

Roger Altman had made a deep impact on Rob and Jane during the time he lodged with them. Naturally, when an opportunity arose for Rob to pay some of this kindness back, he was absolutely delighted. In 1995, Roger invited Rob to become a trustee for the charity he ran based in Carmarthen. They worked together eagerly, but then they were to receive some devastating news. Roger received a cancer diagnosis, and in under a year he sadly passed away. Rob was heartbroken and felt the loss greatly.

Although it was an immensely difficult time, Rob saw the grace and provision of God in the year that had gone before. Due to the circumstances, the trustees of Roger's charity found themselves needing to close it down. They needed someone business-minded to help. Thankfully, that person would be Rob. Having had enough time to learn about the charity and apply his business experience, he was able to sensitively make the necessary arrangements. In doing so, the peace of God and His hand in the details were felt readily. Rob felt it an honour to be able to do this service for his much-respected friend, and all those involved felt the overwhelming peace of God in challenging circumstances.

Chapter Seven

A PLACE OF SAFETY

- individual stories -

- Sarah -

Sarah arrived looking downtrodden and tired. She had a devastatingly poor family background and was living in conditions that could only be described as inadequate and unsanitary. Sarah had grown up with a distinct lack of support amidst experiencing learning difficulties. As a family already known to social services, they had experienced previous intervention in order to try and improve their living conditions, but it had not made the required impact. She stood on the doorstep wearing a bright pink shell suit, which was essentially all she arrived with, and so she was taken into the home and given the choice of a bath or a shower. After having a shower and her clothes cleaned, she emerged downstairs, her face radiant with joy.

As the pregnancy progressed, Sarah gained the much-needed input from Jane in terms of learning how to maintain hygiene and basic skills in cooking and cleaning. Once the baby, Adam, had arrived Rob and Jane gave as much input as possible in terms of teaching Sarah how to care for and nurture him. Initially, Sarah seemed to be coping remarkably well. Adam had settled into a lovely routine with all his feeds being on time, until one day the routine evaporated. Feeling perplexed, Rob and Jane tried to determine why there had been such a dramatic shift in capabilities. It became apparent that Sarah had been relying on the daily rhythm of television programmes in order to time the feeds, knowing that she was supposed to give a bottle to Adam when specific programmes were being aired. When the schedule had changed with the seasons, she found herself completely lost, not possessing the skills to tell the time independently.

As the weeks progressed it became increasingly evident that Sarah would not be able to adjust to the consistently changing needs of a baby, something which Jane had to testify to in court. Rob and Jane accompanied Sarah to the hearing. The outcome, not unexpectedly, was that Sarah had to say goodbye to Adam, leaving court without him. Knowing that they had contributed to this mother losing her child at that moment felt immensely painful to Rob and Jane. They endured a very tense and quiet car ride home, with Rob and Jane struggling to find adequate words as they left the courtroom and the child behind.

They sat with Sarah that evening and offered their heartfelt apologies. To their great surprise, Sarah looked straight at them, explaining that she understood that the role that Rob and Jane had in the court case had been done with the best of intentions, going as far as saying, 'It's okay, I know it's because you love me'. This sent a tingle down their spines, as they felt disarmed and undeserving; this had spoken to Sarah more than they could have imagined. Love can often be associated with enabling another's happiness, allowing their desires to be met and avoiding difficult situations in order to protect them from pain. In Proverbs 13:24, however, a description is given that makes it clear that love is expressed through discipline, through the setting of boundaries, careful instruction and guidance. It was within these boundaries that Sarah experienced real love. Rob and Jane received a phone call from Sarah on Adam's birth date for the next few years. He held a huge piece of her heart, and although she did not possess the skills to physically care for him, she loved him nonetheless.

- *Niamh* -

Unfortunately, as well as situations where individuals were not adequately able to care for a child, there were also too many situations where the economic and social position of the family would not allow it, not for the lack of love or ability, but as a result of limited social support. This was particularly the case where there was no involvement with social services and no attached funding.

One such mother heartbreakingly found herself in this position, Niamh, a young Catholic girl originally from Ireland who had moved to London after falling pregnant with her first child outside of marriage. The parents adored their son, Ronan, and worked hard to provide and care for him, bringing him up in a loving family environment. However, when Ronan was five years of age, Niamh found out that she and her partner were expecting another baby. She panicked. She could not abort the child (it went against everything she believed in), but she could not physically afford to care for another child either: they were struggling as it was.

It was this distressing situation that led Niamh to Rob and Jane. It was agreed that Niamh and Ronan would stay with them until the baby arrived, and then they could proceed with the adoption process. Following the birth of her daughter (Maeve), Niamh and Ronan said their goodbyes: to Rob, Jane and Peter, but most painfully to Maeve. After returning home to London the family's economic position experienced a shift. Niamh and her partner found themselves in a much better location, and as a result they became more economically and socially secure. This meant that they had the money and sufficient support to not only care for themselves, but the capacity to care for another – their second child, Maeve.

Due to the rapidity with which their situation had altered, the 'cooling off period' had not yet elapsed: the baby had not yet been placed for adoption. Arrangements were eagerly made for Maeve to be taken home as part of the family. They journeyed back to London, securely holding the daughter they had almost lost. For such a tiny bundle she radiated joy throughout the family. In later years, Rob and Jane attended the wedding of Niamh and Adam. Their hearts swelled with joy at the precious sight of this family, and right at the centre was Maeve: her gentle nature and contagious laughter unavoidable. This was their very vision in action, and they rejoiced at the outcome.

- Lily -

'Call me Lily,' said a beautiful young Asian girl, as she stood on the doorstep of Rob and Jane's home with her bags in hand. She had agreed to move in after being cast out by her family for whom it was not so much the pregnancy that had been shameful, but that it highlighted the sin of sex outside of marriage. The baby therefore, had to be 'got rid of' for her to be accepted back into her family. Lily did not want to place the child up for adoption, still less could she face the prospect of abortion. So, without a home, little choice remained: Lily would live with Rob and Jane while she waited for the birth of the baby. Following the birth of her son, she signed the paperwork handing over her rights to the child, and in doing so secured her readmission into the family.

Sadly, Lily had shared during her stay that due to the shame and nature of her sin, she believed she would not be eligible for an 'appropriate match' when her marriage was arranged. She would be given in marriage to an older man who had already lost his spouse, inheriting a role that could be more accurately described as carer than wife.

Lily called Rob and Jane around six months later to check on the baby, and for the first two years of the baby's life collected the letters associated with him. After that, the communication ceased and it was only possible to surmise the kind of life Lily then led, including whether she had the prospect of ever having a family. What was particularly poignant about Lily's situation was that it highlighted how unaware one might be of another's sufferings. The majority of people who met Lily identified the beautiful, smart young woman that she was, but it was the pain and brokenness that she carried on the inside that defined her. It was a stark reminder that regardless of what is evident, everyone has a story.

- Bonnie -

Without having personal experience of placing a child for adoption, it is perhaps all too tempting to imagine that it is an 'easy' option. This couldn't be further from reality: it takes incredible mental strength and fortitude to willingly act against maternal desires and to choose a life that is deemed more beneficial for the child. This strength was evident in Bonnie (a young mother from Essex). Already mother to another child, whom she had at a very young age, nineteen-year-old Bonnie was simply not in the social situation to be able to care for and house another. She had decided that in order for the child to receive the care they deserved, she would place them for adoption.

Generally, newborn babies are placed into foster care during the 'cooling off' period, before they can be adopted permanently. Bonnie chose a different path, committing herself to caring for her beautiful baby girl, Isobel, for the first months of her life until she could place the child herself into the arms of her forever family. She bravely faced the pain of her own loss, so that she could secure a better life for her much-loved baby.

- Stacey -

Of course, not every mother demonstrates an unwavering devotion to her child. This can become particularly evident as the child grows older and makes mistakes. It was in this situation that Stacey was handed over to Rob and Jane. At sixteen years old, she stood gazing up at this large house in the middle of the countryside, not too far from her home town, yet feeling another world away as she listened to her mother's admission. Her mother unashamedly explained that she would not have her pregnant daughter in the house; she did not love her and therefore, Rob and Jane could have her instead. Having made her statement, she promptly turned and departed, leaving Stacey standing in the open doorway.

As Rob and Jane got to know Stacey, they became aware of some of the ways in which she had sought love and affection. She was a beautiful young girl and had learnt that this made her desirable to others. Knowing that her physical appearance was one of the most significant ways she gained positive affirmation, she frequently flaunted herself in a desire to feel loved. This led to difficult conversations about what was deemed appropriate in the house, but it also served as an opportunity for Rob and Jane to model a different kind of value system to what she was used to. At the same time however, this led Rob and Jane to the realisation that this would also not be a suitable environment for Peter to grow up in as he headed towards his teenage years. Regardless of what Stacey learnt during her stay, she never did have the opportunity for reconciliation with her own mother (she was asked if she wanted to be present for the birth, but declined). Following the birth of her baby, Stacey sought accommodation through the local authority.

- Michael -

Although there were a great deal of difficult moments and great sadness in many situations, there were also glimpses of hope. One of the most remarkable transformations was witnessed in one of the fathers, Michael, whom Rob and Jane had come to know, a man who demonstrated a substantial amount of aggression and agitation. His views on God and his own self-worth were made explicitly clear, as he stated that he would never set foot in a church for fear of being struck down.

One night, he shared with Jane that he felt God had spoken to him through a dream, showing him that he was required to make a choice regarding the course of his life. This was a pivotal moment for Michael, significantly impacting the direction of his future. Jane fondly recalled sharing this conversation with him: being overjoyed at the journey he had taken so far. In a display of joy for him, she leapt up on the bench in the hallway, embracing this 6-foot, previously brusque man, relishing the opportunity to send him on to embrace a new life and a new way of living.

- Maddie -

The family that Rob and Jane created and invited others to share was precious. For many young mothers this would be their first experience of living in a loving family home, and became something they wanted to hold on to. This was what Maddie felt so strongly as a result of her stay with Rob and Jane. She spoke of feeling cared for and protected, acknowledging that Rob and Jane had become parental figures in her life. In desiring to hold on to this, she made a request for Rob and Jane to adopt her. As she was already in her early twenties, this window of opportunity had closed, but it served as a clear example of the impact that caring for those who need support can have: it can be life-changing.

It may not have always been clear to Rob and Jane what impact their love and care had on an individual. Not all of those who came to share their home appeared changed by the experience. But what they did understand was that it was enough to plant a seed and to trust God with the process of softening a heart. In whichever way seemed best for each individual, Rob and Jane sought to sow seeds of love and hope, to show a glimpse of God's goodness that can be present even in the darkest of places.

Chapter Eight

IN EVERY SEASON

- officially Living Springs -

Due to the very nature of what Rob and Jane had undertaken there were undoubtably moments where the situation was overwhelming for the young family. On any given day Jane would care for Peter and be involved with supporting the mothers and children that they were sharing their house with, whilst Rob would be out at work. The evenings did not mark any change in terms of responsibility and workload, with renovations still ongoing in the property and guests living in the same home space.

The charity was still in essence Rob and Jane's home that they had lovingly opened up to support those in great need. But they had become increasingly aware that they had no particular space for themselves, besides their bedroom. This at times felt like a real strain. On one particularly difficult day, feeling physically and emotionally exhausted, Jane decided to rest in front of the fire. On returning with a hot mug of tea to settle down with, she found a resident sitting in the seat, relaxing in front of the flickering flames. The impact of a lack of private space and time to refresh was becoming more evident, and they craved that time as a family and as individuals that would allow them to be nurtured and replenished.

At the same time, it was evident that there was a great need for this space to exist for families, so much so that there was an opportunity to increase the capacity to more than four families. In order to make this a reality they would need to register as a mother and baby home. Due to Peter's age and their need to find some form of separate family environment, Rob and Jane were beginning to realise that their vision had outgrown them and decided to move out. In 1995, they found an ideal home in Kinver. Not wanting to take from the charity, they sold Barratts Coppice Farmhouse for the exact amount they required to move, significantly below what it was worth, but considering it as a gift to the charity. Rob and Jane were only a part of this vision that God had put in motion.

- A mother and baby home -

The process of registering as a mother and baby home put them under the authority of the Care Quality Commission (CQC). Moving out meant that they could take in eight families, and the building underwent a time of work and reconfiguration in order to ensure it best met its new criteria. Jane endeavoured to get everything ready for this change: preparing the policies and procedures, and developing and reconfiguring the staff team, to include a trained midwife. In desiring to maintain the ethos of caring within a community another couple, Peter and Angie Yair, moved into Living Springs to work closely alongside the families. At the official opening of 'Living Springs', Rob became chairman of the trust and Jane was employed as a manager.

Unfortunately, these changes were to have significant ramifications financially. When opening in 1996, there was a real difficulty in making the charity viable. The situation could only be described as desperate, with borrowings totalling £318,000. Already at this early stage, redundancies had to be made and decreases made in the general working hours of other employees.

Following the brutally difficult months of trying to negotiate finance, Rob and Jane felt that they were given a word from God. They felt God's promise that he was walking alongside them through a verse which became a reminder of hope: *this year you will eat what grows by itself, the second year what springs from that. But in the third-year sow and reap, plant vineyards and eat their fruit* (Isaiah 37:30). The message seemed to be that here was a future that would be more abundant… there was hope.

In a later meeting the trustees analysed the finances, highlighting a £28,000 deficit for being able to pay wages that month. Without the ability to pay staff, Living Springs would have no alternative but to close. This was held up in prayer to God, in the trust that He was holding all of the answers. At the time this took place, there was another local charity which had also had to make the difficult decision to close. They had ended with surplus money which they had decided to split between two chosen charities. Rob received a phone call explaining that one of these charities was Living Springs. When the gift arrived, Rob saw in sheer amazement the sum of £28,000: the exact amount required at the time to cover the wages.

- *Up and running* -

As Living Springs took form, a whole new variety of opportunities became available. With a full staff team, they were able to offer a wider array of opportunities to the families that stayed on site. They worked as a staff team to continue to build on the ethos that Rob and Jane had established of family life and care being the centre of all they do. It was a particular pleasure to see families gathered together in the summer months for BBQs, and later in the year for bonfire night celebrations, Christmas fayres or carol singing.

There was a specific focus on building parents up, with the intent that they would be better equipped to care for their families from the point of leaving the mother and baby home. Living Springs provided budgeting, shopping, menu planning and cooking sessions, enabling families to establish healthy routines that allowed self-sufficiency in family life. Due to the fact that many of the families were impacted by their socio-economic position, they were also offered access to education, job training and benefits advice.

The relationship between parent and child remained at the heart of Living Springs, and consequently play sessions were also offered. This enabled parents to spend quality time playing and doing crafts with their children. This was not only an extremely valuable time spent together building relationships, but also modelled what family life could look like for them after moving on from Living Springs. Emotional support would be offered in a similar vein: analysing family dynamics and the impact on parents and child alike. The desire was for families to achieve long-term change, which required holistic support for health and healing.

Alongside the paid staff, Living Springs also treasured a team of committed volunteers, who either assisted in running the classes or simply befriended the residents. For Rob and Jane this was a simple demonstration of God's love to those who needed it most, in the way that Jesus calls his followers to be like salt and light to others (Matthew 5:13-16).

There is a sense of scepticism around the possibility that those who need the kind of help that Living Springs sought to offer could experience real and lasting change. A young woman called Amie was a perfect candidate for that opinion: she came to Living Springs having had six babies previously taken away.

Amie was determined to raise her latest baby and so committed herself with the support of the staff to make the most of the opportunities that were offered. During the stay, she demonstrated the ability to care effectively for the child and left Living Springs as guardian. There was never the opportunity to discover what happened to the family long term, but nevertheless, real hope had been offered where there seemingly was none.

- Prayer Life -

Underpinning everything that occurred at Living Springs was a vibrant and committed prayer group: individuals who felt a burden to pray. The team would pray over the individual rooms before and after use, in a desire for God to be a part of all that happened at Living Springs, asking that God would give each resident a safe and peaceful environment to support them in their journey. Such was the felt impact of the prayer group that it wasn't unusual for unbelieving staff to request prayer over specific rooms that they felt uncomfortable staying in, or bring personal prayer requests for difficult home circumstances. In fact, the prayer group would receive regular requests for prayer from staff, residents and even social workers who were associated with the charity.

One father, Jason, who became aware of these prayer meetings during his visits, requested to attend. He took the opportunity to ask for prayer and described feeling a tangible sense of peace. Jason then went on to enquire about christenings, seeking to find some of this peace that he had experienced for his daughter in the future.

As the charity evolved, situations arose that challenged the trustees in their responsibility to their faith. Within the setup of the mother and baby unit, partners had been allowed to visit (whether that required supervision or not depended on the circumstances). Initially, this had fitted well with the structure of the home and supported the idea of building strong families.

They then received an application for a mother and a father to reside at Living Springs together. Without doubt, this would be ideal for the child and would demonstrate the devotion of the father. However, it raised the question of whether the trustees would be agreeing to something that undermined their Christian view of marriage. In order to move forward, the trustees needed to come to a unanimous decision. At the first meeting one of them stood against the notion. It was decided that the issue would be discussed again at the following meeting.

By the time the trustees gathered again there was a very different atmosphere. The trustee who had previously held doubts arrived at the meeting eager to share her conviction and peace that this was in line with God's will. She fully supported moving in the direction of offering a place to both mother and father. So, in May 1996, the home became a place for both mothers and fathers to find solace. Following this decision, Sarah and Mike became the first couple to move into Living Springs together as a family unit, with their young child, Sam. Unfortunately, not long into their stay, Sarah made the decision to leave the family. Although this was a particularly difficult time for Mike and Sam, with the support of Living Springs, Mike stayed for a further four months before taking Sam home, fully embracing his role as a single father.

- A series of loss -

Leanne and Ben came to Living Springs having already suffered a great deal of loss. They had recently grieved the sudden loss of a child, through what had been recorded as natural causes. Whilst working with the family, staff developed the view that something did not feel right, particularly with the way in which Leanne behaved. Unfortunately, they could not evidence their views and without that, nothing more could be done. Following the family's departure from Living Springs, staff received the heartbreaking news that the second child had also died.

The staff gathered together at hearing this news and wept for the life of this child that they had come to know and love. In those times of despair and questioning, staff had to rely not only on the sense of teamwork but also on emotional care for each other. There was something precious about the relationship between those working at Living Springs, particularly on occasions where all there was to be done was to cry, grieve and call out to God.

Joanna came to Living Springs during the pregnancy of her second child, having a three-year-old already, whom she loved dearly. The circumstances of this pregnancy however were more challenging: the father of the unborn child was abusive. As much as she loved this precious life that was growing inside her, she knew that keeping the baby would be tying herself and the child to the abusive partner indeterminately. With this in mind, she arrived at Living Springs in order to birth the baby and give them up for adoption to give them a new life... a life of freedom.

Joanna faced this situation with fortitude, being focussed solely on the welfare of the child. An adoption agency was found and adoptive parents identified. Choosing to care for the child herself until adoption could be formalised, Joanna was able to place her beautiful baby girl, Lena, into the arms of her new family, trusting them to give her the life that she deserved. Even though she was fortunate enough to find a wonderful husband and have additional children, nothing filled the space that her daughter, Lena, held in her heart. Thankfully, when Lena turned eighteen, she started the search for her birth mother, enabling them to be reunited and subsequently they formed a strong relationship.

- *Moments of joy* -

Many of the life-defining moments appeared in the seemingly insignificant events, in ordinary day-to-day life. Abigail had been staying at Living Springs for a few months getting used to caring for her newborn baby, Luna. Anyone who has parented is aware of the rapidly changing needs of a small child; on reaching the stage of feeling confident with one particular aspect of parenting, the needs seem to shift again. So it was that on Luna approaching six months, Abigail was attempting the process of weaning, but possessing no cooking experience, this felt like a difficult task.

Sharing her concerns with one of the staff members, Abigail soon found herself in the kitchen: apron on and ingredients ready. Carefully and patiently explaining each step, the staff member encouraged Abigail to complete each stage of the process herself. When they finally gazed down at the steaming hot fish pie, the sense of achievement radiating from Abigail's face left the staff member truly overwhelmed by a love for her job.

Some memories linger forever. One staff member recalled putting together a care package which had been stowed in the cupboard, ready for an occasion where a mother may arrive seeking refuge. The package included the employee's own nightdress and dressing gown. On a later shift, she was surprised and amused at the sight of one of the fathers waltzing around in the nightclothes! As well as bringing great humour, this also served as a stark reminder of the complexities of life. People cannot be reduced into categories: successful or unsuccessful, valuable or not so, positive or negative. In every human, no matter how broken, there is a capacity for joy; all have something of value to offer to others.

- Community Support -

Alongside the work that Living Springs was doing with the mothers who resided with them, they also continued to support the community through the work at the Pregnancy Advice Centre. The centre dealt with a significant range of individuals, aged from fourteen to fifty-one, with the majority being school or college-aged children. When the centre opened, there was a high level of need: pregnancy tests were not readily available and very expensive to buy, and a significant stigma existed around pregnancy out of relationship. Many individuals did not feel that they had a dependable support network where they could get the advice they needed.

During the four hours that the centre was open daily, staff would expect to test and spend time with around five women, being particularly keen to offer them adequate time to support their needs. This could involve offering advice in terms of life choices and contraception if the pregnancy test was negative, or discussing options and provision if the result was positive. It was emotional support that was most important to the staff: they were not simply a practical resource of pregnancy testing, but being present in the chaotic and difficult parts of life. The centre recognised some of the women as fairly regular attendees. Although this highlighted challenges for the individual, it also allowed opportunities for people to be nurtured and cared for.

As society changed, so too did the role of the Pregnancy Advice Centre. Pregnancy tests became more affordable and attitudes towards pregnancy outside of committed relationships had shifted. As a result, many individuals now had other options for support, particularly from their families, meaning there were also an increasing number of young mothers who would decide to keep and raise their babies.

Alongside this, there were also changing views around abortion. In earlier legislation (the Abortion Act 1967), abortions were legalised under set criteria. This paved the way for the 'pro-choice' movement, where pressure was building particularly amongst the women, to claim the right to abort. With the previous stigma of abortion losing some of its potency, there emerged a need to offer post abortion counselling. As a result, the Pregnancy Advice Centre then sought training from CARE, to better equip staff to address some of the trauma issues that had begun to arise. This allowed the centre to provide weekly post abortion counselling to the majority of those that they came into contact with, following a program called 'The Journey' which sought to enable emotional healing.

Roger, Jane, and Rob all deeply valued the counselling services they had established. But policy changes emerged that altered the landscape of the service. Many of the counsellors worked voluntarily, yet regulations had become tighter, with many of them finding that they did not meet the new requirements in terms of paperwork and training and therefore could not continue. This eventually led to the difficult decision that the counselling service within 'The Well' would close. Faced with potential closure of the Pregnancy Advice Centre, Jane rallied a group of volunteers to cover the opening hours. Seeing the value in this service and its impact on the mothers they met, they willingly covered the hours needed to continue the Pregnancy Advice Centre for the following couple of years.

Chapter Nine

THE NEW GROWTH OF SPRING

- contact work -

The running of the residential centre had felt increasingly pressured and difficult. In particular, there were significant challenges around supporting the mental health of some of the residents. Following the regulations set by the CQC, the charity was required to have a qualified mental health nurse on every shift, something they could not feasibly afford.

Upon returning home from a holiday celebrating their 25th wedding anniversary in 1998, Rob and Jane were confronted with the undeniable reality that the live-in aspect of Living Springs had become untenable, and the residential centre closed shortly after. Despite the obvious stress and disappointment, Jane very clearly felt that God was saying, 'But what a great place for a new beginning'. This was not the end of the road for Living Springs; God still had a plan and there was space for new things to emerge.

In October 1998, Living Springs received an offer of contact work from the local council. A group of fourteen children from an extended family had been taken into care and needed regular contact meetings with family (this equated to quite a number of contact sessions per week). As Jane listened over the phone, she dismissed the offer as not being under the remit of their work. However, the moment that she put down the phone, she felt a sense that God was encouraging them to take it on. Knowing that they only had seven staff and that it would be a stretch, she called back and outlined to the council all they could offer. The council gladly accepted and so for some period of time Living Springs' primary purpose became to assist in supervised contact work: offering a comfortable, safe space to allow parents going through complex child care proceedings to spend time with their children. This proved to be successful, so much so that they completed over fifty contact sessions each week. It also brought much-needed finance into the charity, allowing it to gain a much more stable position.

Within this work another opportunity to support children emerged. Living Springs inherited the responsibility of transporting the children to and from the contact sessions. The volunteer attached to each child became a safe person, building relationships of trust over time and creating a space where children felt comfortable to share their thoughts and feelings. They gave comprehensive care to the child during the process of waiting for the parents' arrival and supporting them after the visit, and were also required to put together formal reviews and collate evidence for court on occasion.

- *Supporting the children* -

From the beginning a significant focus of Living Springs was on supporting parents, yet in this new role the light was shone irrevocably on the impact on the children involved. Staff felt the value of supporting parents in making positive memories as a family, positive experiences in the midst of tumultuous times. It was essential that children had happy memories with their parents to look back on and use as a reference point for their own identity, alongside the opportunity to build a level of relationship, in order to bolster their sense of being loved.

During one journey from a contact session, Bethanie shared that she had been scrubbing her skin in the bath to try and whiten her appearance. This was the first time that she had found the courage to discuss her thoughts about her identity and her place in the world. The response to this admission was to seek to affirm Bethanie in who she was: that she was beautiful. The amazement and joy that lit up her face were remarkable to see. In such a minor moment, Bethanie had the opportunity to gain some other perspective on herself. There is something so tangible about love and kindness that even the smallest incidence can disturb the certainty of many negative self-beliefs.

Staff could only do so much, though. Following the separation of the parents of three young children (Samantha and her two older siblings), the family were working with the charity in order to enable contact sessions to take place. Samantha stood eagerly awaiting the arrival of her parent. Every time a car could be heard pulling into the site, she would glance up in hope, only to look away again disappointedly. As time slowly passed, the sounds of arrivals became more infrequent. The emotional toll that this took was understandable, so much so that it affected Samantha physically. As it became evident that no one was coming to visit her, she suffered an asthma attack.

On the occasions where parents did not attend the session, it was the role of the volunteers to care for the child during the allotted time. Some of these occasions would become treasured memories for these children. Thomas sat watching through the sash window for the arrival of his parent. On accepting that no one would arrive to see him, the volunteer staff member endeavoured to make the hour as worthwhile as possible. They wandered down the path to find the chicken coop. Thomas' eyes lit up as he was told that he could go inside and find a newly laid egg. He gingerly picked one out and carried it as gently as if it were the most precious thing in the world. Nothing could entice him to place the egg down for the rest of the visit. It is interesting to wonder why this meant so much to Thomas, why he cherished this in the way that he did, in the midst of his own turmoil. It will never be known, but even so, something of value was given to Thomas that day, and that will always be worth the time invested in him.

- A complex role -

In being involved in the complexities of family life and relationships, there will undoubtedly be difficulties or misunderstandings. Staff would often describe occasions that they needed to navigate that were not necessarily as simple as they appeared. Circumstances varied greatly, and therefore there was no way of creating a specific frame of practice that could be followed. Situations were not always black and white, and therefore staff would inherently need to gain their own wisdom whilst always following the established guidelines.

One of the staff, Michelle, recalls learning an important lesson based on an experience of a split-second decision. She had regularly supervised contact sessions with both mother (Natalie) and father (Steven) of one particular child. Unusually on one occasion, only the mother was present. Michelle was required to take Natalie home before transporting the baby back to foster care. As Michelle pulled up at Natalie's home, Natalie exclaimed that she could see the neighbour outside, and being eager to show off her baby, asked if she could call the neighbour over to the car. In less than the two minutes this had occurred, the neighbour had seen the child through the car window. The staff member had been unaware that the father had had his rights to see the child taken away, and he was furious on discovering that someone else had seen his child. He reported the staff member, and as stressful as this was, it was the opportunity to learn another important lesson: if you're not sure, just say no.

Even with this lesson in mind, issues could not always be avoided. Following another contact session, Michelle was responsible for ensuring a child called Samuel was returned to his foster carers. When she arrived however, she realised that the foster carers were not present, but had left their fifteen-year-old daughter in their place. Deciding this time to err on the side of caution, Michelle requested verbal permission from the foster parents before leaving Samuel in the teenage daughter's care.

Unanticipated by Michelle, this created a high level of anger and offence from the foster father in what he saw as a lack of trust in their biological daughter to care for the child. There were always so many nuances involved that staff had to be ready to expect the unexpected, and to work with grace and a willingness to empathise with people in whichever situation they were in.

Aside from those occasional misunderstandings, Living Springs developed strong relationships with numerous foster carers. There were several children who had been placed in long-term foster care, where the parents had maintained visitation rights. It was those multi-agency relationships that were usually hugely beneficial for the child: having a strong network of individuals who were supporting and offering stability.

- *Intergenerational difficulties* -

The families that entered Living Springs often possessed a myriad of difficulties that prevented them from adequately parenting their children. Whilst these issues had to be addressed as part of safeguarding and supporting the child, it was also vital not to oversimplify the narrative so that a parent simply became a list of wrong choices.

Although it is never acceptable for a child to live with neglect, it is also a type of abuse that can exist entirely without intent. Some parents simply do not have the life experiences themselves that allow an understanding of how to meet a child's needs sufficiently.

This is where generational cycles become increasingly evident: a person can generally only give out of what they themselves possess and often re-enact what they have experienced for themselves. When reminded that many of these parents were living out of their own trauma - unhealthy attachment styles, co-dependency and trust issues - it enabled compassion to grow and a desire to see them succeed, not only for the child's sake, but for the parent's sake too. Many parents came to contact sessions with a desire to learn and improve. Based on their determination and willingness to try new ways of interaction with their children, many contact sessions went well.

It was often the case however that good intent battled against parents' own trauma and difficulties from childhood. Zachary had contact sessions with his father, Rich, a hardy-looking man decorated with tattoos. There was no doubt that Rich loved his son and relished the time he got to spend with him. During the sessions he sat playing alongside Zachary, it became evident that this was exactly what he was doing... he was immersed in building with the Lego, and so emotionally he struggled to connect with his child as he was still finding ways to meet his own childhood needs.

Realising what he was doing, he hurriedly pushed the construction away, creating the perfect opportunity for the volunteers to offer him another biscuit alongside his coffee. Rich stared up in amazement, questioning why he had been offered more. There was something so heart-wrenching about the childlike needs and emotions of parents like him that transcended the space of judgment: they themselves were victims in a cycle of failure.

Technological advances began to impact the sessions as well in the form of dependency on and addiction to social media. For many struggling parents, it became a form of escapism and safety: a platform where life was what you chose to share, a created image and a way in which affirmation could apparently be gained. Being in the grip of social media however, increasingly took away from real-life connections and the ability to face and alter difficult circumstances. This was particularly evident within contact sessions. After the initial greetings, parents would often find themselves lost for words, without ideas on how to interact or build relationship. Social media would act as a safety blanket in those moments: it would not be unusual for screens to replace interaction with their children.

During contact sessions, staff were not permitted to tell parents what to say or how to behave, but had an opportunity to offer suggestions. The majority of the time, these were gratefully received. During one session, Vicki was struggling to change the nappy of her vivacious fifteen-month-old. Following suggestions from the staff, Vicki's face flooded with relief once it became evident that distracting the child with something new meant that they were much happier to lie still during the change. Generally, it is not a lack of effort that leads to these struggles, but the simple fact of having never been shown. Not being allowed to instruct, staff developed a gentle approach of leading by example: loving and speaking to children in a gentle and affirming way, offering support at the expense of their own time or demonstrating empathy and understanding in difficult situations.

Living Springs, for many, became a point of calm and stability, and developed a reputation as such. Family life was often chaotic, and children more often than not felt that impact (even if they were placed in foster care). With the familiar staff and safe environment, Living Springs was a place where families felt at home. They relaxed into a sense of safety that enabled positive connections to be made between parents and children.

- A range of outcomes -

The work of Living Springs sometimes gave an opportunity for outcomes to come to light that were not normally expected. In the case of deciding which parent should be given custody, the court generally leans in favour of the mother. But through being able to oversee separate contact sessions of both mother and father in a non-residential assessment, Living Springs staff were able to deliver accurate representations of both parents' abilities with the child.

This was seen and celebrated in one particular case. James and Talia separately participated in their contact sessions with their child, Ellie. James demonstrated a particularly strong bond with her, and his effective parenting strategies were clear. He consistently gained in confidence and proved his desire to step up for Ellie, and the final decision as to custody went in his favour.

Parents were given the opportunity to learn and change, but ultimately the duty of care focussed on the children: to ensure them a place of safety. And so, there were many cases where the decision was made to remove a child from their birth family altogether. The last contact session prior to adoption was felt poignantly by all involved. Whatever the circumstance, it was impossible not to feel the loss experienced by the birth parents at this time, to not feel empathy for the broken-heartedness and separation that followed. Considering this, Living Springs endeavoured to offer the most peaceful and warm environment possible for these very difficult moments. Cosy spaces were created, with twinkling lights and candles: a way of showing love in the midst of a desperate situation. Life Story Books were completed– a book which told a child's story of origin and a collection of positive memories of their birth family (an essential part of supporting a child to form an identity for later in life). Staff felt the rawness of those moments and depended on and valued the support of the team. And although the situations seemed so desperate and painful, they were encouraged that on the other side of that moment in time, there was to be a new family awaiting the child, offering a positive future.

Although the contact work was extremely valuable, it caused questions to be raised over the usefulness of the residential home. February 1999 was also a difficult time for The Well coffee shop financially, and the trustees saw an opportunity to cover the debts that had been built up through selling the residential home at Living Springs.

This was an incredibly conflicting and confusing time, a time where Rob and Jane faced the potential loss of everything they had sought to build. Yet, they were not alone. Over the many years that they had been serving through their home and as Living Springs, they had shared God's heart in the work that they did. There were many who had seen this and were passionate about its importance. Having these people alongside them, advocating for the residential centre meant that in October 2000 the decision was made to separate Living Springs and The Well into two separate charities, each with its own focus.

- Time to continue -

Having secured the property, staff at Living Springs were keen to forge ahead with its renovation. They set their sights on the old stables. Although in disrepair, they held many wonderful features that the Living Springs team was eager to incorporate within the designs, in order to keep its former charm and identity. Peter Yair played a significant role in this transformation, possessing strong practical skills that benefitted the project. With this in mind, in 2003 the renovation of the Family Room was completed embracing the rustic farmhouse feel: keeping the original beams and repurposing the trough as toy storage space. The Family Room provided a great space to enable families to meet together for contact sessions, but it was also functional as a space to hold training sessions for the wider community.

Because of the flexibility that Living Springs had in regards to pursuing its own aims, there were numerous ways in which families and children could be supported. Staff recall meeting one young boy, Damien, who Jane had come into regular contact with through her part-time job as a Social Worker for Dudley Local Authority. This troubled teen had been expelled from every school he had so far attended. Jane received a call requesting her assistance with a safeguarding risk at a local school. Damien had climbed onto the school roof and refused to move. On Jane's arrival, she summoned him down, to which he acquiesced, but in that moment, he had lost his last opportunity to be educated in any Dudley school.

On seeing an opportunity to break the cycle of his situation, a teacher, Alan Taylor, was employed through Living Springs to support Damien's academic studies in the morning. As a result of his exceptional skill and patience, Damien began to make progress. Alongside his studies, he also had the experience of learning practical skills alongside Peter Yair, who had a particular skill in woodwork and craftsmanship. Many afternoons were spent creating beautiful bird tables. Once Damien was old enough to work, farm work was arranged for him. These interventions made a significant impact on him, and he went on to lead a successful life.

Chapter Ten

STANDING MAJESTIC

- a time of growth -

As time moved into the 2000s, laws and regulations slowly changed, posing yet further challenges for Living Springs. Most significantly was the funding allocation: now the local authority would only cover the costs for the contact session itself and not the cost for mileage and staff hours for collecting the children, leaving Living Springs to inherit the shortfall. Consequently, the contact work proved less and less financially viable.

Due to the changes, it seemed an ideal time to pursue the residential work again. The process was set in motion by the reregistration of the charity, followed by numerous months spent networking and advertising the work that was offered at Living Springs. From this work, the charity received a lot of referrals, particularly from Telford Council and the residential side of the charity again began to flourish. They then received referrals through Dudley MBC for residential placements and support, particularly for emergency placements as there were no other centres that offered the same level of support locally.

- Renovation -

As the residential family work thrived, Living Springs was able to focus again on the purpose of the building: continuing with adaptations which would create additional space. The house had served Living Springs effectively up until this point, but there was an opportunity for growth. Those involved believed greatly in the expansion of Living Springs irrespective of their financial position and therefore, designs were constantly being drawn up; the vision for the entire property expanding.

Next to the family room lay the hay barn: a large open building, with a beautiful archway in both the front and back. It lay dilapidated, barely standing, let alone being anywhere near functional, and yet the team at Living Springs were not deterred. Although the hay barns were the main focus of the renovation, it was also essential to complete structural work on the old blacksmith's building, cattle shed and coach house, which were all in significant disrepair. Although it was not possible to renovate them to a liveable standard, the trustees were keen to avoid additional costs in the future of rectifying continuing deterioration of these ramshackle buildings.

Amidst endless fundraising pursuits and applications for grants, there were many days when the project seemed too overwhelming. But there were incidences where staff felt encouraged to continue the pursuit. As Jane lay in bed one morning, finding the motivation to get up and begin the day, she was struck by a vision like no other that she had ever experienced before. She saw, more clearly than she would ever have expected, a vision of the hay barn with scaffolding around the lower level. This affirmed for her that the building conversion would be completed. In recognition of what Jane and the staff at Living Springs felt from God, they held a thanksgiving evening in the haybarns. The night was bitterly cold, and bats swooped and glided in the dark. The wind rushed through the centre of the building through the two archways, so those meeting to pray had to huddle together at either end of the building.

Living Springs launched into a season of dedicated fundraising. Local patrons demonstrated their support for the charity, which added credibility to the project, increasing the interest from those in the local community. This support from the patrons (Sir Patrick Cormack - MP for South Staffordshire, The Right Reverent Jonathan Gledhill - Bishop of Lichfield, The Reverent Fr. Vincent Nichols- Parish priest of Our

Lady and All Saints Church in Stourbridge, Lyndon Bowring- founder of CARE and Alison Nicholas MBE- Professional golfer and winner of US Women's Open 1997) made a significant difference in the applications for grants and bank loans. It also raised the profile of Living Springs, bringing in support and donations from other local charities and from within the community.

Having raised the necessary funds, the hay barns were spectacularly renovated whilst maintaining their original character. Standing in front of this building, it is impossible not to admire the blend of modernity and country charm, the archways still holding prominent place. The building was made fully accessible, and beautiful French windows overlooked an enclosed garden. More importantly, this building now offered another four self-contained one-bedroom flats to house families, doubling the capacity at Living Springs.

- Pursuing Goals -

The drive and determination of the staff and trustees to see Living Springs flourish motivated the desire to seek training and skills development. Seeing the way in which laws were changing Jane recognised that she would soon be required to hold a level four management qualification in order to continue in her role, and she enrolled on a management course at Halesowen College, achieving the award in July 2004.

Although management skills were essential to the role, it was further social work training to degree level that Jane desired to pursue. She remained dedicated to providing the utmost she could for families through her personal employment as Social Worker and as manager of Living Springs. She set her sights on an advanced degree in Social Work; not only would this bolster her knowledge, but it would also widen the scope of what the charity could offer. The ideal course was identified at Gloucester University, which offered the opportunity to study one day per week over four years. This would allow her to continue working with the families, something she would have been reluctant to step away from.

Following a daylong interview, she felt inspired in her desire to study. But as one of forty-nine applicants applying for only fourteen places, she held doubts as to whether this would be a possibility for her.

Much to her surprise she received the news that she had been accepted on the course. She was elated, but aware that there was still the difficulty of finding the required finance. Not deterred, she contacted a charity which provided grant funding for individuals who worked in the charity sector. They informed Jane that they could offer a grant for the full £4,500 to cover study fees. Not only that, but they also offered a grant to support the purchase of course materials. Jane felt that once again God had orchestrated all the details, allowing this next step to be pursued.

Partway through the course, Jane realised that she had overlooked the need to complete a placement in the third year. In order for this to be possible she needed to employ someone to replace her, a cost they simply could not cover themselves. Knowing that the same charity had assisted them before, Jane decided to ask if there was any way that Living Springs could receive further support. She explained the situation and was asked to specify the required amount of funding. At this point, the receptionist exclaimed in surprise that they had exactly the required amount. She elaborated how they had received a phone call earlier in the day to explain that one of the other students was no longer in a position to complete their studies and had returned their remaining funding: the exact amount that Jane had requested. This not only benefitted Jane, but the charity too: being required to allocate the funding by the end of the financial year. Jane completed the course and graduated in 2008.

As an acknowledgement of all Jane had achieved, she later received an MBE in 2011: a well-deserved recognition for the fifteen years she had dedicated to creating a safe haven for over six hundred vulnerable families. Rob felt incredibly proud of what Jane had achieved as a first-hand witness to the time and dedication that Jane had devoted to this work.

- Development of the Courtyard -

The charity had settled into its role of residential work, relishing the extra space that the hay barn conversion had allowed, alongside benefiting from the study that Jane had undertaken. It seemed the ideal time to turn their attention to the next phase of redevelopment.

What had been the blacksmith's workshop and cattle shed had become one singular building, which stood adjacent to the old coach house. Having previously been structurally renovated, the buildings brimmed with new potential. So it was that in October 2010, an application was submitted to the Social Enterprise and Investment Fund for the £129,000 needed to complete the building that had been named The Courtyard and the Coach House. Living Springs also launched into a time of fundraising to secure as much finance as they could going into the renovation.

They had already located the individual who they wanted to undertake the job, an experienced local builder with whom they had connections through church. So strongly did they feel God's peace that they would be granted the money for this project that they actually commissioned the project to begin in January, before receiving any confirmation that they would be allocated the funds. They received a phone call between Christmas and New Year to explain that a grant of £110,000 had been allocated to them, ten days before the work was to commence.

- Individualised Support -

Living Springs had embarked on a remarkable journey of growth over the previous twenty years, bringing ever more opportunities for those needing support within the community. Initially, Rob and Jane had sought to support pregnant mothers in finding alternatives to abortion. But alongside this remaining focus, the scope had also widened. The desire was to support families, but with a specific emphasis on reaching those for whom the experience of family involves an element of suffering:

abuse to the child from either parent, abuse to a spouse, parental neglect perhaps due to mental illness, drug or alcohol abuse. Taking those circumstances into consideration, the families were taken in and offered support to allow the parents to become more secure, safe and healthy for their children.

Regardless of the specific work that Living Springs offered there had never been a 'one size fits all' approach, and priority was given to organising holistic care, specified to meet each family's individual needs: the heart of the charity was to walk alongside each individual in the midst of their suffering. As a result, there were mothers who were residing at Living Springs in low level supervision housing as a route to adoption. But there were also families who required more intensive support, such as Isobel who was in the process of recovering from a drug addiction in order to refocus on her family, and on a daily basis she would arrive at the office in order to receive her methadone treatment. Living Springs staff were keenly aware of the necessity of supporting a parent's recovery alongside maintaining and promoting the welfare of the child.

With such a wide variety of situations and social backgrounds, there was always an element of uncertainty. 'Red alerts' were commonplace, forcing the centre into lockdown to ensure the safety of the residents. And yet staff regularly remarked on the lack of fear, describing instead a sense of peace and safety. Psalm 23:4 perfectly encapsulated their experience: *even though I walk through the darkest valley, I will fear no evil, for you are with me.* There were never any attacks made on staff or attempts at vandalism, substantiating the belief that God was protecting them.

This sense of peace seemed to hover over Living Springs. Staff and residents regularly commented on the tranquillity that could be experienced there. Never more so than in the early morning: the sky often became tinged with a pink hue as the sun began to climb up into the sky, allowing the hedgehogs and foxes to be seen frolicking before scurrying away as the light stole away their starry cover.

- The place of faith -

As with any organisation, Living Springs was moulded by changes in policy and subsequent guidelines. Most significant to the staff at Living Springs were the restrictions on sharing religion. From the outset, Rob and Jane had invited people into their home where they could freely share the love of Jesus and offer prayer, but this had rapidly been eradicated. Conversations about Jesus were only permissible if initiated by the mothers themselves. It could at times be a challenging issue to navigate, as much of what the staff were committed to doing was hinged upon demonstrating the love of God; it felt only natural that this should be evident in the work they did.

The prayer life of the charity became even more integral as a result of these changes, forming a substantial part of the daily rhythm. For Jane and the prayer team it was a journey of steadily trusting God at every point, holding the vision lightly and repeatedly offering it up to Him. During those times they regularly experienced the closeness of God. One lady, a committed member of the prayer team, regularly shared images that she felt were from God. The team treasured these images: they stirred their spirits, motivated and buoyed them, especially during challenging times.

One image in particular became a firm affirmation that God was still present in the work at Living Springs. The image was that of a tapestry. At first look, the tapestry was simply a myriad of knots and cast-offs: it was a mess. But on turning it around there was a beautiful, perfectly woven picture. It communicated to the team that even in the midst of the messy situations they faced, the difficulties and painful circumstances, God was creating something greater and more beautiful than what could be seen. It gave hope that even when things looked bleak, God had a plan, and they were reminded to keep their focus on the bigger picture.

It was the endeavours of the staff to demonstrate love to those with whom they worked, which often caught the attention of the families. One evening shift, a staff member was supporting a young mother, Abbie, and her young baby, Sophia. Due to safeguarding concerns, the child was not permitted to be alone in a room with the mother, so a staff member accompanied the baby to a nearby room. Sophia became very unsettled and was taken through to Abbie. In that vulnerable moment, Abbie began to pour out her life story: the lack of support, direction, and a sense of helplessness. Abbie then looked straight into the eyes of the staff member and questioned 'Why do you do this?', permitting an opportunity to share the love of Jesus, and the hope that can be found in Him.

With support Abbie worked extremely hard while at Living Springs, making significant progress and eventually leaving to continue her parenting journey in the community. Once she had returned to her familiar environments and relationships, however, she began to falter, eventually making the decision to give up the child. This was sadly very typical. Even where the will to parent existed, the snares and pressures of returning to unhealthy lifestyles would invariably prove too challenging.

Even so, all of the families that resided at Living Springs were remembered and cherished. After the families had moved on, they received visits from staff to check on their well-being and were offered additional support for the transition. The families were not just a temporary project to the staff at Living Springs: they were individuals who were fearfully and wonderfully made (Psalm 139:13-15). Displayed on the wall in the office were photographs of all the parents and children who had spent any time living within the home. They were precious, valued and loved, and staff continued to pray for each and every one.

Chapter Eleven

PRUNING THE BRANCHES

- working within a framework -

Living Springs received an increasing number of referrals from the Local Authority in circumstances where there were parenting concerns and therefore, questions over the safety of the child. These placements were funded by the Local Authority and required reports on the families' parenting capabilities.

Due to the fact that these assessments would be used in court, the procedures became even more rigid. When families first arrived, they would be allocated a set period of time (as determined by social services), during which staff could offer constructive intervention, modelling a variety of parenting skills and providing input into the relationship development between parent and child. Once this time was over however, the staff had to follow a very different approach.

Following the induction period, there was no further scope for providing support and offering guidance, as this would have been viewed as an interference with the accurate assessment, which would have had ramifications in court. This led to a change in the atmosphere at Living Springs. The much-loved day trips with the residents soon had to be left behind, and each conversation had to be meticulously recorded. Staff were encouraged to take a step back, allowing parents to demonstrate their abilities without prompting or guidance, intervening only in cases where safety was in jeopardy. Their role was to observe and write up reports, becoming accustomed to a specific way of detailing what they observed, ensuring they displayed no bias or laid claim to anything they could not substantiate.

During these assessments, parents were required to demonstrate their capabilities in managing their own self-care and that of the child: creating a predictable routine, ensuring basic needs were met with adequate meals and clothing, and managing appointments with outside providers such as health visitors. As it was an assessment, every aspect of care needed to meet the detailed criteria set by social services. For example, regarding feeding, there was a specific way of preparing the bottles for the babies, a particular bottle cleaning technique, and a specific fridge temperature. Individuals had to be very mindful to follow the criteria without variation in order to demonstrate their capability.

Initially staff were viewed with suspicion, as though they were only there to inform social services of misdemeanours. This led the staff to feel they needed to go above and beyond to show a different attitude toward the families: working as a team, demonstrating care and creating a loving environment. Over time, staff were able to build positive relationships even in this challenging context and they became trusted to assess fairly, recording all the moments of positive parenting as well as documenting the difficulties. This allowed Living Springs to become a safe place where many individuals felt comfortable. Families were assessed monthly, meaning that the length of stay was indicative of the effort parents were willing to make to keep the family together. Some were prepared to stay for over a year to demonstrate their desire and capability.

Living Springs was also able to extend its reach within the community. In 2013, the charity employed a community worker, which enabled it to offer community-based parenting assessments through visitation in families' homes, offering parental support within the community as well as holding the ability to assess the eligibility of caring relatives. The charity also took on ownership of a two-bed flat locally (in Wollaston), which families could move into following a residency at Living Springs. This allowed extra time to support a positive transition back into community: an opportunity to find appropriate housing and identify supportive community networks whilst maintaining the support of Living Springs within the process.

Due to the links with The Well in Stourbridge, Living Springs was also able to use the space above the coffee shop in order to host coffee mornings, creating a space for people to stay connected to their support networks. This community role was vitally important. It was at the point of returning to their own communities that parents often began to falter, struggling to apply their new skills in the midst of their previous social circumstances. Having someone to reach out to for support was vital in giving families the opportunity to retain good habits and healthy relationships.

As assessment work continued to shape the life of the charity, Rob realised that he had become more distant from the family work within Living Springs. As his main work was still within the family business, he was not directly involved in these assessments. As a result, he did not participate in the same training as the staff and eventually found that he could not speak to residents for the risk of jeopardising a court case. Rob continued to focus on the finances and project management of the charity, but he felt that there was a separation or disjointedness that he had not experienced before.

- OFSTED -

Tightening up every aspect of the assessment work was a change in policy which resulted in Living Springs being placed under OFSTED supervision (The Office for Standards in Education, Children's Services and Skills) in 2013. Alongside criteria set by social services, the staff were now bombarded with a checklist of protocols which impacted every aspect of the charity's work.

Alongside this, staff also felt a further tightening of restrictions around religion, particularly regarding the sharing of Christian beliefs – a trajectory that was felt increasingly over the following decade. An example of the felt direction of these restrictions was the legislation that has been passed (but not yet enacted) in order to forbid silent prayer in the vicinity of any abortion centre, something which Rob had done faithfully and respectfully in support of his own Christian and pro-life beliefs. It felt to some that society was becoming more paradoxical, in a culture that had become increasingly accepting of every individual: their beliefs, sexual orientation and identity, there seemed little room for Christian beliefs and attitudes to be held individually in the same way.

Even so, Living Springs pursued their work wholeheartedly. Jane took responsibility for overseeing the court reports, due to her high level of Social Work training, demonstrating a particular skill in detailed and clear record keeping. Being academic, she could be relied upon to ensure that the assessments were of high quality and robust enough for court, as well as possessing the organisational skills needed to meet deadlines, even during periods of high workload. She regularly correlated twenty-page reports, which she then presented in court proceedings. This residential assessment was the final opportunity for the parents to demonstrate their capability before a decision was made regarding whether the child would be removed from their care. The majority of these situations sadly resulted in the removal of the child from their parents. Staff had to be intentionally mindful not to view this as a failure, praying that it instead created a chance for a more loving and stable environment for the children.

- A time of change -

There was no doubt that Living Springs was doing good work, but the charity also looked completely different to when Rob and Jane first registered their home with CARE in 1989. Living Springs had been serving the community for over twenty years, holding a fantastic reputation with social services and other agencies, but they began to experience feelings of uncertainty, as though the foundations of the charity were beginning to crumble. This triggered a particular time of questioning over the future of Living Springs. It wasn't that Rob, Jane and others involved had turned against what they felt God wanted. It was more like walking a route one degree in the wrong direction. At first it doesn't make much of a difference, but at the end of a long journey you find yourself increasingly far from the place you began.

It became important to consider options for the future of the charity as Jane approached her retirement. Over a period of time, she deliberated on what this would look like both individually and for the charity moving forward. Eventually, the decision was made that the deputy manager would take Jane's place as manager. Having demonstrated her capabilities and understanding of the charity whilst working together, Jane felt sure that she would lead the charity in the right direction. This therefore, allowed Jane to retire from her full-time work in May 2019, after thirty years of hard work and dedication. Jane continued to work a few hours a week, only fully retiring in February 2022 at the age of seventy.

In amongst these changes a friend and leader in their local church, John Cook, increasingly got involved, initially offering support, but over time taking on more responsibility within the charity. He worked alongside Jane in order to understand how things ran and gain insight into what the charity could potentially offer within the community. John became an integral part of the charity, later becoming its chief executive in 2018.

Together, they searched for ways to bring Living Springs back to its roots of Christian support within the community. Yet it became increasingly clear that this desire was not compatible with the work that it was involved in. As well as this concern, the assessment work became increasingly difficult to maintain. Numerous small assessment centres had been forced to close due to difficulties with funding, as they simply did not bring in enough finance to make it viable: it was the bigger organisations that were succeeding. The way in which some charities had negated these costs was to move towards lower staff budgets: relying on CCTV for twenty-four-hour supervision, and staff overseeing multiple families. Not prepared to make those sacrifices and lose their people-centred approach, the assessment centre was forced to close, and staff were made redundant. For a while, Living Springs lay dormant.

During this time Living Springs was visited by two Christian ladies who listened to the journey of the charity and its current position and expressed that they believed Living Springs had suffered from 'mission drift'. This reflection resonated; it was evident how local authorities had taken ever-increasing control over how Living Springs operated, not least in the way in which sharing the love of God had become severely limited, even within a Christian charity.

For Living Springs, the slate had been wiped clean. No longer under OFSTED or tied to a specific role, they could reshape and reform the charity. John (chief executive), Rob (chairman of the board) and the trustees spent time praying and seeking clarity over the direction the charity should take.

- Personal Impact -

In this period of dormancy, Rob and Jane reflected on the life that they had given to Living Springs, not being able to escape the phenomenal impact that this had on them individually, not only practically, but also emotionally and spiritually. At the beginning of their journey, they had little awareness of what it would entail, seeking to rely completely on the assurance that God had called them and therefore, would guide and equip them. This was a daily commitment to trust (even when situations looked bleak and hope seemed lost) and to actively turn towards God - a life of repentance, turning from sinful ways and repeatedly choosing to walk in the ways that God would desire. Often it was difficult, but in the end, something always seemed to change in the most unexpected ways. Rob and Jane always felt the truth of God's promise to answer, even before He is called (Isaiah 65:24).

Rob and Jane's hearts were to live the life that Jesus called His people to, and modelled Himself walking with the broken, the hurt and the struggling. It is in those places that individuals can most profoundly walk with Jesus – a kind of intertwining of spirit that allows God's glory to be revealed to His followers and for them, in turn, to reflect the glory of God.

For Rob, as he journeyed in his faith, he learnt about the goodness and grace of God and through this revelation of what is truly good and loving, an awareness was formed of where he himself had fallen short. As he began to learn something of the love of God as his Father, he became aware that he had not given all he could to his own son, Peter. One morning, Rob expressed the desire to share with Peter some of the family history and its impact on his life. Father and son walked side by side to Aunt Tabitha's grave and to the Chapman's tomb. Rob opened his heart to his son, discussing those who had held meaning in his life. He took the opportunity to apologise for where there had been a lack of presence in Peter's life as a father, where time was spent absent through work or sport commitments: time that would have been spent differently if the choice was given again.

For Jane, her faith had been tried and tested to the point of no denial. She had witnessed and felt God's presence so closely. During one time of testing and struggle, Jane recalled calling out to God in desperation with the acknowledgement that she wasn't sure she believed He even existed anymore. But what had gone before was undeniable, and in the next breath, Jane heard herself utter, 'Even if you don't exist, God, I can't help but love you.'

Chapter Twelve

REMOVING THE IVY

- supported housing -

After a period of searching and trusting in God for the way forward for Living Springs, it was eventually decided that it should be taken back to its roots of dedicated personal family work. Anna Burdon was employed as manager to support the implementation of this vision. Sharing the ethos of what Living Springs stood for, Anna flourished in her role. Living Springs moved into providing social housing for families in crisis in a community-based environment. Underpinning its ethos were the seven principles of incarnational living, which asked staff to seek a way of life that involved serving others and living out the attributes of Jesus as a way of service to Him.

- Incarnational Living -

The first of the principles is a connection to God the Father. When Jesus walked on earth, He made the time to spend with Father God; this connection was critically important (Mark 1:35, Matthew 14:23). This time spent seeking God can quite easily be the first thing that gets left behind when lives are busy and time is limited, but it must be a focal point if it is to be the guiding theme of everything else. For the staff involved in supporting the families in Living Springs, there is a desire to stay connected with God. Twice a week they pray together, one of those times being open for residents to attend or send prayer requests to. Staff are committed to keeping God at the forefront of what they do.

Once this is central, the second principle flows naturally – living with a purpose. It is not enough to wander round aimlessly, or even live with a checklist of things to achieve. There has to be a purpose underneath it all. At the most basic level, Christians are called to share the truth about God in the same way Jesus did (John 18:37). It is when individuals act with a clear purpose that their actions most plainly reflect that. Staff at Living Springs are united by the purpose of serving God in His desire and passion for the redemption of families.

When Jesus lived on earth He spent the majority of His time with sinners, the poor and the broken. He spent time amongst His family, friends and the apostles, supporting each other in community living (John 3:22). As the third principle of incarnational living, this is where His followers should be: dwelling among the people. This underpins the whole ethos of Living Springs: walking alongside others. In fact, from the beginning it was the shared living that had the most impact through the relational, emotional and practical support that was freely offered. It often was in the minutest of details of daily life that the families residing at Living Springs felt most loved and blessed.

Up until this point, someone may live like this from a relatively safe position: to do and say the right things. Yet, God calls believers to open themselves up for the sake of others: to engage authentically (as the fourth principle requires). Jesus always connected with His followers. He demonstrated compassion for those who suffered (Mark 6:34) and was affected by others' emotional distress (Luke 7:13). In short, Jesus acted as though those around Him really mattered, and He calls His followers to live in the same way. So, as the families reside at Living Springs, staff commit to journeying with them in an open, relational way: to be authentic in their care and compassion in order that the families may feel the love of God through them.

The fifth principle sets the direction for all of these actions. It is to serve 'the least of these'. Jesus sought out the marginalised, the sick, the rejected and the hurting - it was those people who needed Him the most (Mark 2:15-17). He didn't do this by handing out money to them. He walked with them and touched them. Living Springs is built on meeting the needs of those who have found themselves in situations of difficulty. The staff have made the commitment to walk alongside those who are struggling and hurting.

Jesus was keen to call people to Himself, and as the sixth principle of incarnational living sets out, that is part of His followers' role too. Jesus on many occasions would call people to follow Him, and was clear that this required a level of sacrifice and commitment. Due to the openness about the faith-based ethos of Living Springs, there is great scope for sharing the love of God with families. Staff are open about what faith and commitment to faith look like for them, and all are welcome to attend church with them if they wish to.

Finally, these principles in action should bear witness to those around and call them into the same way of living. It should cause others to want to live as the principles of incarnational living describes. There are various ways in which Living Springs does this. With the residents, the staff seek to demonstrate a way of living that is authentic and more desirable than they may have experienced before. This often causes those individuals to question why the people and the atmosphere are so different to what they are used to. Additionally, in the wider community, Living Springs inspires and challenges others to consider what they could offer and how living differently in their day-to-day lives could make a significant impact.

In summary, the seven steps of incarnational living require nothing other than what is already required of anyone who loves God. Christians are not called to give out of the surplus of luxury. Instead, the instruction is to be openhanded towards the poor (Deuteronomy 15:11), feeding them and clothing them, giving the homeless a place to stay (Leviticus 25:35), having the willingness to do as Jesus did, to share in the sorrow and suffering of others, to weep with those who weep (Romans 12:15). It is the great commission: to be sent as Jesus was sent, to be a witness to God's love (John 20:21) in the hope that God will draw in the lost (John 6:44).

- *Family Chaplains* -

As Living Springs found its new rhythm, John began to wonder whether they were now in the position to have a family living within the community. With this in mind, John was reminded of a local couple who had previously expressed an interest in community family work.

In 2018 a local couple, Tim and Liz Barton, also part of the same church as Rob, had become increasingly aware of their call to serve families within the community. They couldn't escape their conviction that meeting someone for an hour a week was simply not enough to see transformation in individual lives. They dreamt of finding a place where they could live alongside struggling families, in community with them, walking through life together. Having been aware of Living Springs they thought that this could be the place for that vision to become reality, and so they wrote a proposal, outlining what they felt they could offer. However, due to the formality of the assessment centre the proposal was rejected, the concern being that the couple's role would have interfered with accurate and objective assessments.

Tim and Liz were approached by John to give them an opportunity to rediscuss their vision and how this could be woven into the fabric of Living Springs. They spent time praying to try to discern God's will, alongside meeting with Rob and Anna. Together, they formed a vision, debating various aspects of their role, their living arrangements and discussing what could be achieved for the residents. As a result of this period of prayer Tim, Liz and their three children (Lucas, Jesse and Lillianna) moved into the Coach House to live alongside the residents.

Tim and Liz became Family Chaplains, in the hope that their desire to serve in faith was clear from the beginning. Christians can be viewed negatively in society- either outdated, self-righteous or just plain weird. Tim and Liz wanted to demonstrate a different reality, seeking to be a living example of giving time, seeking change, raising happy children within healthy boundaries and making sacrifices for the good of others.

They were also keen to be distinguished from the paid staff, allowing them to build the necessary rapport to live communally with the residents. Very quickly they fell into their daily rhythms, having constant contact with the residents, walking through the difficult times in their lives. They found that it was through informal conversations that relationships were strengthened, rather than through scheduled meetings. It was as they had always expected: in order to make a significant difference, they needed to be living in community with the people they wanted to support.

- God's grace -

Tim and Liz reflect on the blessings they experienced in undertaking this role. They have often been amazed by the grace of God evident in many situations, particularly that families that were so receptive to them in their first months. This allowed them to feel confident in the vision, which bolstered them in more challenging times. The occasions where they walked with families and journeyed with them to faith they count as a pure gift from God, relishing sharing baptisms and testimonies of change and hope.

There were, of course, difficult times; not every individual was as receptive or trusting of Tim and Liz's intentions. It was deflating to invest significant time in someone, only for them to make negative assumptions or react to them personally for decisions that were out of their control. Because of confidentiality, Tim and Liz could rarely defend their decisions to others, but it was in those difficult times that they felt the love and peace of God so closely.

It is human nature to want to defend and explain a decision or contest one believed to be wrong. But for Liz particularly, she felt that she needed to surrender her control over her reputation: trusting that God would put truth and honour on display. She experienced this repeatedly, finding that residents would apologise for wrong assumptions or accusations without the need for Liz to defend her own position. God not only protected her reputation but also highlighted the integrity and grace with which they are seeking to live by.

Tim and Liz relished their role, but it was particularly in the unexpected moments that they were most impacted. One evening a meeting was held for the residents to attend. As a mark of community, the decision was made to cook a meal for all the families to share beforehand. One of the mothers, Tandy, looked down at the meal, and in amazement looked back at Liz remarking that nobody had ever cooked for her before. Liz felt somewhat taken aback. In her eyes, she had only cooked a simple pasta bake and hadn't even considered the meal as any kind of outreach, yet it had demonstrated so much more to Tandy.

Another mother, Melissa, had lost everything in a house fire before moving into Living Springs, so she possessed nothing with which to furnish her new property when the time came to move on. The staff had given this need to God in prayer and began to search for some of the items she would need. Partway through this process, Living Springs received a phone call: a man had intended to move to the area and had fully furnished a property, but the situation had changed, and he no longer required any of his furniture. He was calling to enquire if there was a need he could possibly donate to: a whole house's worth of brand-new furniture and appliances. Melissa was overwhelmed (as were the staff) by both this significant gift and God's provision and timing.

Tim and Liz's life has been indelibly marked by their decision to follow the call of Jesus to live communally with families. It has drawn them closer to God, increased their capacity to love others and given them a greater sense of the purpose of life. Even more incredible is that they have shared this with their own children. Tim and Liz realised that Lucas, Jesse and Lillianna had their part to play too. They have demonstrated love for the children they come into contact with and treated them well, demonstrating positive relationships with others and within their family.

There are many stories that illustrate the impact of this, but none more so than the journey of David and Aliyah...

- David and Aliyah -

David and Aliyah were living their dream life: financially stable, living in a beautifully well-kept four-bedroom house. They had created a loving family with three long-term foster children who were so settled that they referred to David and Aliyah as Mum and Dad, and their young biological daughter, Summer. Nothing could prepare them for the turn that their life would take overnight and the upheaval of all they knew.

Alongside this family David had four daughters from a previous relationship, which had unfortunately broken down to the point of him having no contact with the children. Unexpectedly, Isabella, David's eldest daughter, attempted to get in touch with him despite this being forbidden by the mother. As a result of this attempt at contact, David then received news of an allegation made against him which was so serious that it altered everything in their lives.

Due to the severity of the allegations, David lost his job, and the foster children were immediately removed, meaning that Aliyah also lost her source of income. In one moment, they lost their income, house, family and reputation. The sense of grief was so intense that it threatened to overwhelm them, particularly from the loss of their foster children.

They moved into a rented accommodation, first depleting their savings and then being forced to sell their assets. Knowing they could not afford the next month's rent, they contacted social services for support. The only advice they received was to wait until they got evicted, something that did not feel right to them given their positive relationship with the landlords. So, on discussing the situation with them, the contract was terminated and they were given a few weeks to find somewhere else to live.

Aliyah's brother, Christopher, kindly allowed them to stay with him for a couple of months. So, the majority of their belongings were locked up in storage and they lived with minimal space. This became more challenging with the arrival of Isabella, who had again reached out and came to live with them. A couple of weeks later however, the situation was to become untenable. David received a phone call from his previous partner, informing him that she would be placing the two younger girls, Willow and Lily, in his care as well.

Staying with Christopher was no longer feasible, and so social services found accommodation for them in the form of a room in a Travelodge. Their situation was nothing short of desperate. Aliyah and David now shared one room with four children, two of whom had just arrived from their mother's care in quite a poor condition mentally, physically and emotionally. Willow and Lily were also afraid, not just of their new circumstances but of their father himself, given how he had been portrayed to them by their mother. David and Aliyah were completely depleted in every sense of the word.

- Finding a place -

On returning to the Travelodge one evening, they were informed that the arrangement to stay in the room had not been renewed by social services and therefore all of their belongings had been removed and placed into a laundry bin. Thankfully, a place was found in another hotel not too far away, but the reality was that this was a family living at crisis point.

A short while later social services got in touch to say that they had found a more permanent residency: a place at Living Springs. On viewing the property, David and Aliyah took the manager by surprise with the declaration that they needed to move in that evening, as they had nowhere else to go. So, a few hours later the family moved into a two-bedroom flat in the Courtyard. The three eldest, Isabella, Lily and Willow, living in the one bedroom; and David, Aliyah and Summer in the other. Every piece of unnecessary furniture was removed to allow them space to sleep. Yet, for now, it was stable and safe.

Unfortunately for Isabella, the location and feel of Living Springs triggered too many memories of her previous rural upbringing, and being aware that it was not working for her, she made her own arrangements to leave. The rest of the family spent the next five months at Living Springs. It was an intensely difficult time both for Aliyah and David and for the older children: journeying the loss they had all felt, attempting to establish new relationships and attempting to recover from some of the trauma they had experienced.

Moving into Living Springs was not an instant solution for all their problems, but they reflect on the positives of what they experienced and the impact this had on their lives. The most tangible difference for the family was the sense of community. It wasn't unusual for all the residents to be outside together, children splashing in the paddling pools and laughing as they played together. With challenging circumstances in common, the families would prioritise these times together as a way to cope and to provide the best experiences they could for the children. The charity also had very clear guidelines on the responsibilities the families held for their own children, and the need to respect the privacy of personal space within their own rooms and accommodation, enabling a sense of safety that the family relished.

It was during this time that Tim and Liz were spending increasing amounts of time at Living Springs, establishing their role as Chaplains, before they officially moved in. Over the following weeks, Aliyah and Liz in particular began to build a relationship. Liz was able to share her faith with Aliyah, who was open to ideas of spirituality. So, when Liz invited Aliyah and her family to church, it was a fairly easy decision to make. Not only would it support Aliyah in her exploration of faith, but it would provide an escape from their environment and circumstances. It was also an opportunity for the children to spend time with others their own ages. For these reasons, the family continued to attend church over a series of weeks.

On one particular Sunday, the family were having a slow morning, but Aliyah made the decision to attend church alone. Severely struggling with her mental health, she stood during the worship, absolutely broken and desperate. A member of the worship team shared her belief that there were mothers in the room who needed to know that they were enough, that they were seen and they were appreciated. To Aliyah it was as though this was being spoken directly to her, addressing every doubt and fear that she had failed her children through the circumstances she had found herself in. Full of emotion, and removing herself from the room, she unexpectedly found herself in the arms of a woman, assuring her that she was the daughter of a king and that she was more than enough in God's eyes. Aliyah was blown away by the love she experienced and what she had felt: a very real sense of belonging and worth. It wasn't difficult to see that Aliyah had been deeply touched by this encounter. On returning to Living Springs she shared this with Tim, who wept beside her as she described the way she felt she had 'come home' through experiencing the Holy Spirit.

David was also experiencing an intense low point in his life. He was full of guilt for the way his past relationship had affected every aspect of family life, painfully aware that the blame for Aliyah's mental health struggles was firmly placed on him, and daily witnessing the unhappiness he felt he had caused. In every way he felt defeated and broken.

On the following Sunday, the family again attended church. David stood while the church worshipped. They began singing 'In my Father's house, there's a place for me'. Feeling touched by this David turned to share his feelings with Aliyah, only to see her singing and smiling in worship. He immediately felt as though God was saying to him that he too belonged. In that moment he felt wanted; something he had not felt in an agonisingly long time. For David, he would describe this as his 'pulling moment', where he would begin to seek the heart of Jesus.

As the family learnt more about faith, they acknowledged that whilst life and suffering are intertwined, they were not alone. In John 13:33, Jesus states, *In the world you will have tribulation, but take heart; I have overcome the world.* There is a future hope that is promised to those who believe. But believers are not abandoned in the present: God promises to walk alongside, to be near to those who call on Him (Psalm 145:18). This family began to testify to this, experiencing God's presence amidst overwhelming darkness. Aliyah still battled with her mental health, at times feeling suicidal. Willow likewise struggled to process the trauma that she had experienced throughout her childhood. It felt as though a smothering darkness lay over them. One day in sheer desperation they felt the need to escape, so they bundled the family into the car just to walk to the top of a hill in the pouring rain, desperate to breathe and lay their despair before God. In that moment a dripping wet man, hunched against the rain, strode purposely towards them. He stopped, looking them straight in the eyes and said to them that God had put it on his heart to tell them that they belonged to God and that everything was going to be okay. In that remarkable moment they surrendered their lives to God, trusting that they were in His hands. The next day, David received the news that the allegations made against him were dropped and his name had been fully cleared. For the first time in a long time, opportunities lay ahead of them.

After several months, the family were offered council housing and moved away from Living Springs, but they continued to reflect on the impact that Living Springs had on their lives. For the children, they particularly valued the outdoor space and the autonomy it gave them to explore and play. It offered them a sense of freedom and connection to nature within safe boundaries. David and Aliyah testify to the experience of community for those who have become completely isolated. Many families residing in Living Springs had found themselves detached from any sense of social support, an experience which could be life-altering. Finding people who care, who are willing to journey through painful situations, allows the time and safety for families to stop, to contemplate and most importantly to explore and pursue better options. It is a circuit breaker for families that are willing to reflect and desire change. That was certainly true for David and Aliyah, as it has been for many others.

- *The next stage* -

In offering supported housing, Living Springs has been able to support many families. In order to ensure this continues, the decision was made to seek support from a larger charity: YMCA (Young Men's Christian Association), a charity dedicated to promoting the spiritual, intellectual, social and physical welfare of young people as well as being deeply rooted in Christian values. Therefore, on 1st April 2025, Living Springs was reformed and renamed – YMCA Living Springs. Being managed by YMCA gives greater opportunities for access to funding and therefore offers security for the future. The larger organisation also provides greater opportunity not only for the staff in terms of training and support, but to widen the scope for the charity's future growth.

In reflection of the journey of Living Springs so far, there is no telling what the charity can achieve as it continues. From the tiny seed of an idea given to a couple in the midst of pain emerged a wide-reaching charity offering support within the community for struggling families. Although what Rob and Jane achieved is remarkable in building the foundations of the charity, they have always been keen to ensure that the accolades are rightly placed with God; they also recognise that they were merely workmen in a God-designed plan which far exceeded themselves. They acted on what God had given them, but it was due to Him that the charity grew and flourished. It was the love of God that enabled Living Springs to become the refuge and place of safety that it is.

Rob, Jane, and so many others who have been involved within the charity to date speak fondly of what they have gained from their involvement. It is this richness which resonates; it is not what each one has given or achieved, but what they have experienced in the process of attempting to follow God. The joy of walking through the woodland and catching glimpses of golden light dancing through the trees. What an honour to walk in that light.

It is also a lesson to those who follow Jesus to be able to hold any work for God lightly. It ultimately belongs to God, and when it is clear that individual strength has faded, there is nothing more honourable than to hold that work open-handed and allow others to continue the legacy.

There have been many involved in the journey of Living Springs, and all have been touched in some way by God's grace and goodness. But every individual has only played a part, contributed to each chapter. The story of Living Springs is entirely God's, and He has not completed it yet.

THE END

Rear of Haybarns as first visited before deterioration took place.

Rear of Haybarns as first visited before deterioration took place

Laying of new electric and water mains.
The day Rob came to the Lord.

Work started on the Courtyard floors and externals.

Start of the work on the Haybarns.

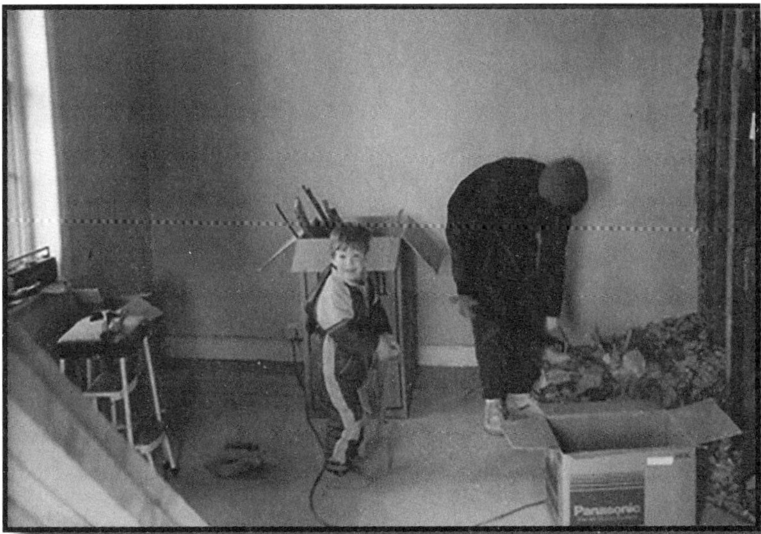

Jane and Peter labouring once more in the Main House.

Deterioration of the front of the Coach House 1995

Deterioration of the rear of the Coach House 1995

Deterioration of the building before finance available 1995.

Stage 2 of the front drive laying with scalpings spread mostly by Jane, with a little help from Peter.

Finished externals of Courtyard and construction of Coach House underway.

Haybarns consisting of four one-bedroom self-contained flats. 2015.

Main House and community rooms containing two two-bedroom flats. 2015.

Aerial photo taken in 1990
before the deterioration of the buildings.

Artists impression of completion. Part of an appeal for funds to complete Courtyard and Coach House internals.

Staff and volunteers in 2007.

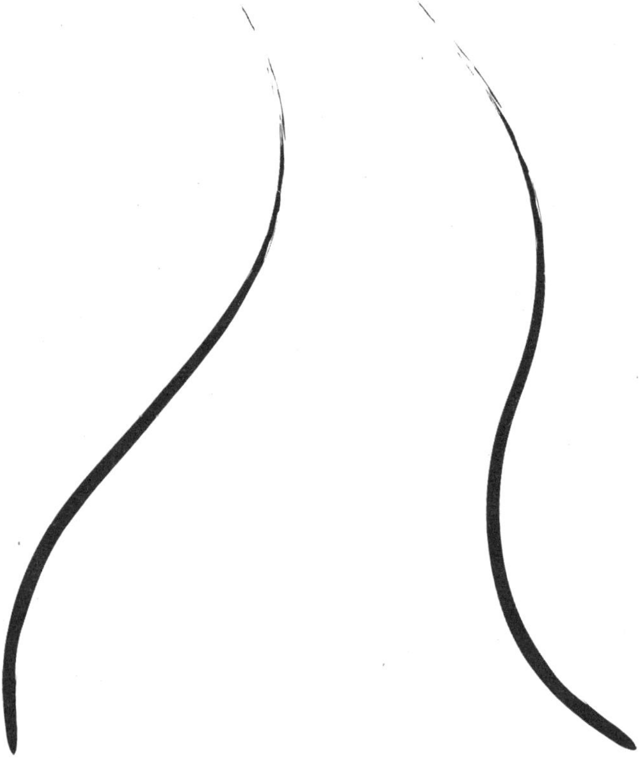